Michelle Obama

IN 1985, MICHELLE OBAMA TURNED IN HER SENIOR THESIS, AN OFT-CITED WORK WHEN REFERRING TO HER LIFE AND ACCOMPLISHMENTS DESPITE BEING THE WORK OF A YOUNGER WOMAN.

BILL O'REILLY SAID, ABOUT SAID THESIS:

I DON'T WANT TO GO ON A *LYNCHING PARTY* AGAINST MICHELLE OBAMA UNLESS THERE'S EVIDENCE, HARD FACTS THAT, SAY, THIS IS HOW THE WOMAN REALLY FEELS... THAT AMERICA IS A BAD COUNTRY OR A FLAWED NATION... WE'LL TRACK IT DOWN.

"PRINCETON-EDUCATED BLACKS AND THE BLACK COMMUNITY" EXAMINED THE DEBT THAT UPPER CLASS BLACKS FEEL TO LOWER CLASS BLACKS. CLASS GUILT, FOR LACK OF A BETTER WORD, AT HAVING SUCCEEDED. RACE GUILT, AS WELL.

CRITICS MISINTERPRETED AND MISQUOTED HER ACTUAL THESIS TO HAVE A SEGREGATIONIST BIAS, A HARD SELL GIVEN MICHELLE'S ATTENDANCE OF AN INTEGRATED SCHOOL AND HER CHOICE OF ASSIMILATION AT PRINCETON.

MICHELLE'S THESIS CONFRONTED THE WAY SUCCESSFUL BLACKS FEEL TOWARD OTHER BLACKS IN THEIR COMMUNITY. SHE CONFRONTED THE PERCEIVED DEBT THE RICH OWE TO THE IMPOVERISHED. THAT, PREDICTABLY, MADE RICH PEOPLE UNCOMFORTABLE.

SOME HAVE GONE SO FAR AS TO SUGGEST THAT IT IS HER DIABOLICAL PLAN, ONCE HER HUSBAND IS IN OFFICE, TO GIVE A FREE RIDE TO ALL MINORITIES.

OTHER CRITICS SUGGEST THAT HER "ELITISM" DRAWN FROM A LIFE OF EASE AND MONEY GIVE HER NO PERSPECTIVE OF WHAT IT MEANS TO BE POOR, BLACK OR OTHERWISE.

THIS MAN, FRASER ROBINSON, WERE HE STILL WITH US, MIGHT BEG TO DIFFER, AND HE IS WHERE MICHELLE'S STORY STARTS.

HE IS MICHELLE OBAMA'S FATHER, AND HE STARTED HIS SUCCESSFUL WORKING LIFE AS A JANITOR.

MICHELLE ROBINSON GREW UP ON THE SOUTH SIDE OF CHICAGO IN THE YEARS OF INTEGRATION AND WHITE FLIGHT. SHE WAS BY NO MEANS RICH. SHE WAS, AS MOST OF US ARE, MIDDLE CLASS.

SHE WAS BORN SIX MONTHS BEFORE THE CIVIL RIGHTS ACT WAS SIGNED INTO LAW, AS GREAT CHANGES WERE BEING MADE TO THE WAY THAT WHITE SOCIETY REACTED TO BLACKS, AND VICE VERSA.

SHE TOOK THE EL TRAIN FOR UP TO TWO HOURS A DAY AS A CHILD...

...AND EARNED A MEMBERSHIP IN THE NATIONAL HONOR SOCIETY AT WHITNEY M. YOUNG MAGNET HIGH SCHOOL, GRADUATING SALUTATORIAN IN THE SAME CLASS AS SANTITA JACKSON, JESSE JACKSON'S DAUGHTER.

SHE WORKED FOR HER ACHIEVEMENTS. DESPITE NOT STARVING OR LIVING ON THE STREETS, SHE WASN'T HANDED SUCCESS. NOR WAS SHE GIVEN A FREE RIDE.

IF YOU ACTUALLY READ MICHELLE'S THESIS, IT SHOWS A PROFOUND INSIGHT INTO A SENSE OF DUTY TOWARD THE LOWER CLASS IN GENERAL, AND THE BLACK LOWER CLASS IN PARTICULAR.

BUT MOSTLY IT'S STATISTICS GARNERED FROM PERSONAL REPORTS.

HER CRITICS, WHO CALL HER A SEGREGATIONIST, IN THIS RESPECT FAIL TO NOTE HER TIME WORKING PRO BONO FOR THE WORKING POOR...

...ENCOURAGING WHITES AND BLACKS TO LIVE TOGETHER AND BREAK DOWN BARRIERS.

I ENCOURAGE YOU TO READ IT.

MICHELLE GREW UP IN THIS BRICK HOUSE. THE FAMILY STARTED IN THE BUNGALOW AND EVENTUALLY, THE HOME WAS BEQUEATHED TO THEM.

AT FIRST MICHELLE SLEPT IN THE LIVING ROOM NEAR HER BROTHER CRAIG, WITH A SMALL DIVIDER TO SEPARATE THEM. THIS SERVED TO PREVENT HER RICH ELITISM FROM TAKING HER OVER UNTIL SHE REACHED A POSITION OF POWER.*

*THIS LAST STATEMENT MAY BE THE WRITER BEING SARCASTIC/ PARODYING EXPECTATION.

MARIAN ROBINSON, MICHELLE'S MOTHER, MANAGED TO STAY AT HOME, A LUXURY FOR MANY STRUGGLING BLACK FAMILIES AT THE TIME.

MICHELLE'S FATHER WORKED HIS WAY UP TO A CONSUMMATE SALARY DESPITE BEING AFFLICTED WITH MULTIPLE SCLEROSIS.

ONE OF MICHELLE'S JOYS WAS PLAYING THE PIANO, WHICH SHE DID WITHOUT PROMPT FOR LONG PERIODS OF TIME.

FRASER WAS A DEMOCRATIC FUNDRAISER AND AN ACTIVE POLITICAL FORCE IN HIS COMMUNITY. THIS HAS BEEN CRITICIZED AS HOW HE GOT HIS JOB.

MAYOR DALEY WAS THE HEAD OF DEMOCRATIC CHICAGO AND A CONTROVERSIAL POLITICAL FORCE AT THE TIME. HIS TENURE OVERSAW A MYRIAD OF CONTROVERSIES, WHICH MICHELLE'S FAMILY WITNESSED AND SURVIVED.

DALEY PRESIDED OVER THE RIOTS AFTER THE DEATH OF MARTIN LUTHER KING, WITH RUMORS OF AN ORDER TO "SHOOT TO KILL" FROM HIS OFFICE FANNING FLAMES.

IF FRASER GOT THE JOB THROUGH CRONYISM, I THEN PONDER, WHY A JOB AS A JANITOR? WHY NOT A BUREAUCRAT? THEY CERTAINLY MAKE MORE MONEY.

CORRUPTION AND CRONYISM RAN RAMPANT IN THE ALDERMAN SYSTEM, AND EVENTUALLY CHICAGO WAS EXPOSED FOR ITS MACHINE POLITICS, DRIVING CHANGE.

IF FRASER WAS REWARDED WITH A JOB FOR BEING POLITICALLY ACTIVE IN HIS COMMUNITY, IS THAT WRONG? I WOULD THINK INSTEAD WE WOULD TARGET THE MACHINE OVER THE COG, BUT THEN, THE COG ISN'T TRYING TO CHANGE STATUS QUO.

MICHELLE WENT TO PRINCETON IN 1981, FOLLOWING
HER BROTHER CRAIG. SHE SPENT A GOOD DEAL OF TIME IN
THE THIRD WORLD CENTER, WHERE SHE STROVE TO ACHIEVE
CULTURAL DIVERSITY AND EQUAL REPRESENTATION FOR ALL.

HER BROTHER CRAIG
SERVED AS A ROLE MODEL
AND OFFERED MICHELLE A
SOCIAL IN. HE ALSO PLAYED
A LARGE PART IN KEEPING
HER HAPPY AND SAFE.

AT THE THIRD WORLD CENTER,
MICHELLE GOT TO SEE A SPEECH
BY FAMED CIVIL RIGHTS LEADER
ROSA PARKS. SHE FOUND SOCIAL
IDENTITY AND INTEGRATION IN WHAT
WAS AT TIMES A VERY SEGREGATED
SCHOOLING EXPERIENCE.

SHE ALSO GOT TO HEAR THE LAST LIVING MEMBER OF THE
SCOTTSBORO BOYS, WHOSE TRIALS HELPED ENSURE THAT BLACKS
GOT INTO JURIES. IT ALSO ENSURED APPROPRIATE REPRESENTATION
FOR DEFENDANTS OF ALL COLORS DESPITE SOCIAL PREJUDICES.

MICHELLE TOOK CARE OF THE CHILDREN OF UNIVERSITY WORKERS FOR HER WORK STUDY, DEVELOPING HER LOVE FOR THE YOUTH SHE ENCOUNTERED.

ONE OF MICHELLE'S FAVORITE ACTIVITIES OF THE PRESIDENTIAL CAMPAIGN WAS READING TO STUDENTS, UNDOUBTEDLY SPRINGING FROM THESE EARLY EXPERIENCES.

DESPITE THESE OUTLETS, MICHELLE STRUGGLED TO FIND HER OWN SOCIAL CIRCLES, OFTEN WALKING IN CRAIG'S SHADOW.

SHE'D GONE FROM *YOUNG HIGH SCHOOL*, A MAGNET SCHOOL WHICH PRIDED ITSELF ON DIVERSITY, TO A UNIVERSITY THAT STILL STRUGGLED WITH AN OLD BOY NETWORK.

NOW, CRAIG'S STILL A SUCCESS, WORKING AS A BASKETBALL COACH AT OREGON STATE. BOTH WORKED TOGETHER AS A FAMILY TO ACHIEVE GOALS IN AN OFTEN HOSTILE WORLD.

HE INTRODUCED MICHELLE AT THE 2008 DEMOCRATIC NATIONAL CONVENTION.

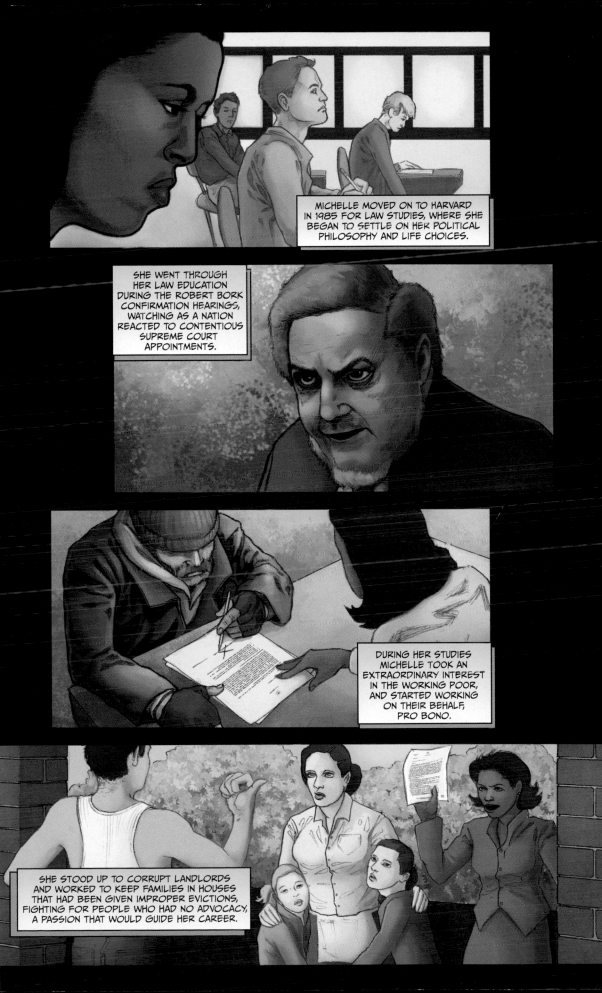

MICHELLE MOVED ON TO HARVARD IN 1985 FOR LAW STUDIES, WHERE SHE BEGAN TO SETTLE ON HER POLITICAL PHILOSOPHY AND LIFE CHOICES.

SHE WENT THROUGH HER LAW EDUCATION DURING THE ROBERT BORK CONFIRMATION HEARINGS, WATCHING AS A NATION REACTED TO CONTENTIOUS SUPREME COURT APPOINTMENTS.

DURING HER STUDIES MICHELLE TOOK AN EXTRAORDINARY INTEREST IN THE WORKING POOR, AND STARTED WORKING ON THEIR BEHALF, PRO BONO.

SHE STOOD UP TO CORRUPT LANDLORDS AND WORKED TO KEEP FAMILIES IN HOUSES THAT HAD BEEN GIVEN IMPROPER EVICTIONS, FIGHTING FOR PEOPLE WHO HAD NO ADVOCACY, A PASSION THAT WOULD GUIDE HER CAREER.

MICHELLE SPENT A LOT OF HER TIME ON THE LOWER FLOORS OF THE GANNETT HOUSE PREPARING LEGAL AID AND ADVOCATING FOR FAMILIES IN POVERTY, PAYING RESPECT TO HER WORKING CLASS ROOTS.

IN CONTRAST, BARACK OBAMA, HER FUTURE HUSBAND, WORKED AT THE SAME PLACE, BUT ON THE UPPER FLOORS AS THE HEAD OF THE HARVARD LAW REVIEW. THEY DIDN'T KNOW EACH OTHER AT THE TIME.

THE CORPORATE MENTALITY FRIGHTENED MICHELLE. NONETHELESS, HER FIRST JOB WAS IN CORPORATE ENTERTAINMENT LAW, MARKETING GROUP WORK. SHE FELT THE DRIVE TO SUCCEED, BUT HADN'T FOUND HER PERSONAL ROUTE TO IT YET.

SHE REPRESENTED A BROAD SERIES OF ENTERTAINMENT INDUSTRY ENTITIES, UP TO AND INCLUDING A CERTAIN PURPLE DINOSAUR WE DON'T WANT TO GET SUED FOR DEPICTING CASUALLY.
LOOK, KIDS! IT'S JOSH, THE ARTIST!
HOT! HOT! HOT!
GOD! JOSH! I'M SO SORRY! I HAD SUCH GOOD INTENTIONS!
MT
MICHELLE MIGHT HAVE BEEN THE ONE QUESTIONING THE PREVIOUS IMAGE'S LEGALITY IN COURT HAD SHE STAYED AT SIDLEY & AUSTIN, THE PRIVATE FIRM SHE STARTED AT OUT OF HARVARD.
THANKFULLY FOR POOR JOSH HERE, MICHELLE LEFT THE FIRM IN 1992 TO PURSUE HER DREAM OF WORKING WITH LOWER INCOME COMMUNITIES.
PHEW! A PATRON OF THE ARTS! A LOVER OF HUMANITY AND BOHEMIA ALIKE!
I'LL PUT YOUR *HEAD* IN THE BLUE WATER FOR THIS, BAILEY!
BUT NOT BEFORE MEETING THE FUTURE PRESIDENT WHEN HE JOINED THE FIRM IN 1989. SHE WAS ASSIGNED TO ADVISE AND MONITOR HIM, A ROLE SHE PROBABLY DIDN'T REALIZE WOULD LAST HER ENTIRE LIFE...

WHEN HER CO-WORKERS ASKED HER ABOUT BARACK, SHE SCOFFED, INDICATING THAT SHE DIDN'T WANT TO DATE HIM. SHE THOUGHT HIM NERDY, AND BY THEN SHE HAD TWO YEARS EXPERIENCE ON HIM.

THOUGH SHE AND BARACK WERE NOT THE ONLY BLACKS AT HER FIRM, MICHELLE DIDN'T WANT TO FALL INTO THE STEREOTYPE OF BLACKS STAYING ONLY WITH BLACKS, AND FELT UNCOMFORTABLE SOCIAL PRESSURE BEING WITH BARACK.

YOINK!

DISAPPEAR'D!

SHE WENT TO GREAT LENGTHS TO AVOID THE FUTURE PRESIDENT, UP TO AND INCLUDING INTRODUCING HIM TO OTHER WOMEN IN AN ATTEMPT TO SCARE HIM OFF.

BUT BARACK WOULD NOT BE DETERRED BY A WOMAN WITH HIGH STANDARDS. INSTEAD, HE WOULD RISE TO MEET HER STANDARDS.

THERE WERE BUMPS ALONG THE WAY. THEY WENT TO "DO THE RIGHT THING" AS THEIR FIRST MOVIE DATE. DESPITE ITS POIGNANCY, IT'S NOT A ROMANTIC FILM.

THE FAMILY WAS SURE THAT BARACK WOULD NOT SURVIVE MICHELLE'S METICULOUS NATURE. SHE'S DESCRIBED AS A WOMAN WHO DOES NOT SUFFER FOOLS AND EXPECTS EXCELLENCE.

BARACK WON POINTS, HOWEVER, BY EARNING CRAIG'S APPROVAL WITH HIS SPORTSMANSHIP IN BASKETBALL, WHICH CRAIG USED TO ASSESS BARACK FOR HIS SISTER.

HE THEN SURPRISED HER WITH AN ENGAGEMENT RING AT THE CONCLUSION OF A MEAL, AFTER PLAYING INTO HER FEARS THAT HE'D NEVER BE READY FOR MARRIAGE.

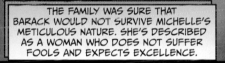

Divorce Rate 346%

SHE PUSHED HIM TO MAKE THE RELATIONSHIP GO SOMEWHERE, AND AFTER TWO YEARS, BARACK SEEMED UNWILLING TO COMPROMISE. HE PLAYED UP MARRIAGE AS SIMPLY AN INSTITUTION.

THEY WERE MARRIED IN 1992 AFTER THREE YEARS OF COURTSHIP.

JEREMIAH WRIGHT PERFORMED THE CEREMONY AT TRINITY UNITED CHURCH OF CHRIST, WHICH PROVED TO BE A POINT OF CONTROVERSY IN BARACK'S PRESIDENTIAL CAMPAIGN, GIVEN WRIGHT'S QUESTIONABLE SERMONS, LEADING BARACK AND MICHELLE TO RENOUNCE HIM AS A PASTOR AND LEAVE THE CHURCH.

FOR MICHELLE THESE EARLY YEARS OF THE 90S WERE A TIME OF VOWS AND RENEWAL OF LIFE. THEY WERE ALSO TIMES OF TRAGIC LOSS. FRASER, HER FATHER, DIED ON THE WAY TO WORK IN 1991.

IN THE SAME TIME PERIOD, SUZANNE ALELE, MICHELLE'S FRIEND FROM COLLEGE, DIED OF LYMPHOMA, PROMPTING MICHELLE TO RE-EXAMINE HER CAREER. DID SHE REALLY WANT TO REPRESENT CORPORATIONS?

ULTIMATELY MICHELLE LEFT SIDLEY & AUSTIN TO PURSUE JOBS THAT PAID LESS, BUT PROMOTED SERVICE, MOVING MORE AND MORE INTO POLITICS WITH HER HUSBAND.

MALIA ANN, THEIR FIRST DAUGHTER, WAS BORN ON THE FOURTH OF JULY, 1998.

NATASHA, AFFECTIONATELY KNOWN AS "SASHA," WAS BORN IN 2001. THEY CHANGED MICHELLE'S LIFE FOREVER, AND THRUST HER INTO EVEN MORE RESPONSIBILITY.

OBAMA'S POLITICAL AMBITION WAS NOT EASY ON THE FLEDGLING FAMILY, AND LED TO PERIODS OF LONELINESS AND FRUSTRATION FOR MICHELLE. SHE WORKED A FULL-TIME JOB AND HAD TO DEAL WITH AN AMBITIOUS WEEKEND FATHER.

AS THE COUPLE FIGURED OUT HOW TO DEAL WITH BARACK'S OBVIOUS DESTINY AS A PUBLIC SERVANT, THEY STRUGGLED WITH HIS DUTY. HE DID HIS BEST, BUT MICHELLE WAS NOT ONE TO SETTLE FOR ANYTHING LESS THAN BEYOND THE BEST. IT'S HER NATURE.

ULTIMATELY, LIKE THE WIFE OF MANY POLITICIANS, IT BECAME A QUESTION OF WHAT SHE VALUED MORE, HER HUSBAND'S CONTRIBUTION TO SOCIETY, OR SANITY. SHE GOT A HOUSEKEEPER AND DID HER BEST TO HAVE HER CAKE AND EAT IT TOO.

MICHELLE BECAME A LIAISON FOR THE UNIVERSITY OF CHICAGO HOSPITALS IN 2001, SERVING LOCAL CITIZENS IN AN ATTEMPT TO CREATE A BETTER INTERACTION BETWEEN POOR RESIDENTS AND LOCAL HOSPITALS, WHERE TENSIONS WERE TIGHT.

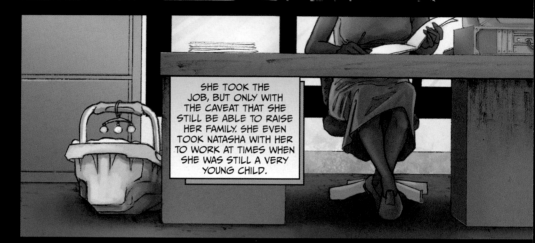

SHE TOOK THE JOB, BUT ONLY WITH THE CAVEAT THAT SHE STILL BE ABLE TO RAISE HER FAMILY. SHE EVEN TOOK NATASHA WITH HER TO WORK AT TIMES WHEN SHE WAS STILL A VERY YOUNG CHILD.

BARACK NEEDED TIME, AND MICHELLE NEEDED BARACK. IT WAS VERY STRAINED FOR THE COUPLE, AND ACCOUNTS INDICATE THAT THEY WERE BARELY ON SPEAKING TERMS, WHICH IS PROBABLY POLITE.

WE'VE ALL BEEN IN STRAINED SITUATIONS. THE COUPLE STRUGGLED TO COPE WITH THE TIME DEMANDS. BARACK BELIEVED HE COULD BECOME A UNITED STATES SENATOR, AND PUSHED FORWARD INTO A CONTENTIOUS RACE FOR A SEAT IN 2002.

AT ONE POINT BARACK TOOK SEVEN DAYS OFF IN A PERIOD OF EIGHTEEN MONTHS. THE FAMILY MADE THE BEST OF WHAT TIME HE HAD, BUT HIS TIME RUNNING TOOK ITS TOLL ON THE FAMILY, AND MICHELLE.

ONE VACATION MAY HAVE COST BARACK THE SENATE SEAT IN 2002. HE MISSED A GUN CONTROL VOTE FOR HIS CONSTITUENCY TO BE WITH HIS FAMILY, AND THE RIVAL CANDIDATE'S SON WAS THEN TRAGICALLY GUNNED DOWN.

OBAMA LOSES SENATE RACE

BARACK STEPPED BACK A BIT, AND SPENT SOME TIME WITH HIS FAMILY, BUT HE NEVER LOST HIS AMBITION. MICHELLE HAD TO WALK THE LINE OF AIDING HER HUSBAND'S AMBITION AND TAKING CARE OF HER FAMILY, AN UNENVIABLE TASK.

HER PATIENCE AND EFFORTS PAID OFF WHEN SHE HELPED BARACK WIN HIS SEAT IN THE SENATE IN 2004, A FAR CRY FROM HARDLY BEING ABLE TO GET A RENTAL CAR FOR THE 2000 DEMOCRATIC CONVENTION.

I LOVE MY COUNTRY, AND I AM PROUD OF IT WHEN IT IS GREAT, AND ASHAMED OF IT WHEN IT MAKES POOR DECISIONS. WE ALL ARE. IT'S A GAFFE THAT I DON'T THINK DENIGRATES HER LIFE AT ALL.

IN THE WAKE OF ECONOMIC CHAOS AND A TOUGH POLITICAL CAMPAIGN, TO EXPRESS PRIDE FOR A HUSBAND AS A POINT OF HOPE SEEMS, TO ME, SMALL POTATOES.

BUT HEY, MAYBE IT WAS UN-AMERICAN AND AWFUL. MAYBE WE SHOULD ALWAYS BE PROUD OF OUR COUNTRY UNQUESTIONABLY.

LORD KNOWS, THAT'S NEVER LED TO ANY CHAOS, SUFFERING, OR PAIN, HE SAID/WROTE IN SARCASM.

MCCAIN'S WIFE, CINDY, WAS QUICK TO JUMP ON HER GAFFE, AS WERE NEWS SOURCES. THE FAITHFUL OPPOSITION LOVES TO VILIFY PEOPLE FOR MAKING A GAFFE. SOMETIMES WITHOUT PAYING TOO MUCH CLOSE ATTENTION TO THE MIRROR.

I AM PROUD OF MY COUNTRY!

I ASK YOU TO CONSIDER WHAT HER COUNTRY WOULD HAVE IN IT, THE COUNTRY PALIN SPOKE OF AS "REAL" AMERICA, A DIVISIVE TERM, WHILE CRITICIZING MICHELLE AS A SEGREGATIONIST.

CONSIDER FURTHER THAT PERHAPS THE ELECTION OF 2008 WAS A STRONG REFUTATION OF BLIND NATIONALISM WITHOUT CRITICAL THOUGHT.

OR MAYBE YOU DON'T AGREE, AND WOULD CARE FOR A CHUCKLE IN THE FACE OF HUMAN MISERY.

IF SO, HERE'S A SING-A-LONG:

♫ BOMB, BOMB, BOMB! BOMB, BOMB ♫ IRAN! ♫

THE GREATER SIN IS YOURS TO DECIDE, I'M JUST SHOWING BOTH SIDES OF THE COIN HERE. JOHN MCCAIN IS A GREAT MAN. HE MADE A MISTAKE TOO. WE ALL GAFFE. IF MICHELLE WAS NOT PROUD OF THIS COUNTRY, WOULD SHE SERVE IT SO PASSIONATELY? SACRIFICE HER FAMILY? HER PRIVACY?

EIGHTEEN
MILLION VOTES.

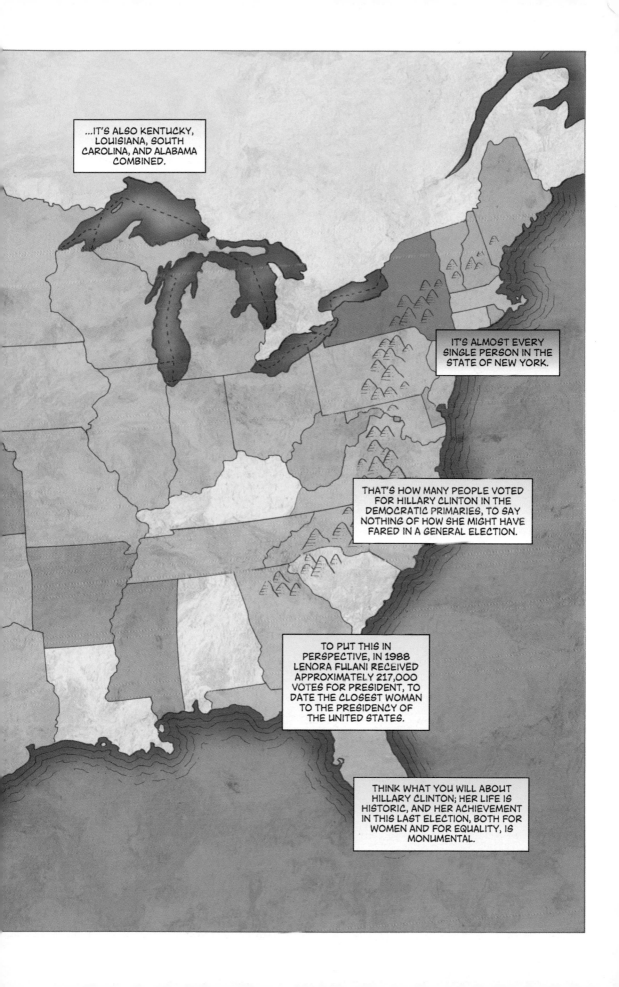

...IT'S ALSO KENTUCKY, LOUISIANA, SOUTH CAROLINA, AND ALABAMA COMBINED.

IT'S ALMOST EVERY SINGLE PERSON IN THE STATE OF NEW YORK.

THAT'S HOW MANY PEOPLE VOTED FOR HILLARY CLINTON IN THE DEMOCRATIC PRIMARIES, TO SAY NOTHING OF HOW SHE MIGHT HAVE FARED IN A GENERAL ELECTION.

TO PUT THIS IN PERSPECTIVE, IN 1988 LENORA FULANI RECEIVED APPROXIMATELY 217,000 VOTES FOR PRESIDENT, TO DATE THE CLOSEST WOMAN TO THE PRESIDENCY OF THE UNITED STATES.

THINK WHAT YOU WILL ABOUT HILLARY CLINTON; HER LIFE IS HISTORIC, AND HER ACHIEVEMENT IN THIS LAST ELECTION, BOTH FOR WOMEN AND FOR EQUALITY, IS MONUMENTAL.

SHE GREW UP HERE, IN A HOUSE HOWARD ROARK MIGHT HAVE RESENTED FOR ITS BLOCKINESS, ADOPTING HER FAMILY'S VALUES AND GROWING ENAMORED OF GOD AND COUNTRY.

IT MIGHT SURPRISE YOU TO LEARN SHE THEN BECAME A REPUBLICAN, GIVEN HER HISTORY AS A DEMOCRAT.

SHE WORKED FOR THE GOLDWATER CAMPAIGN IN 1964 WHEN SHE WAS JUST A TEENAGER.

HE LOST TO LYNDON JOHNSON, BUT SHE REMAINED A REPUBLICAN, EVEN INTO HER COLLEGE YEARS.

IN THE WAKE OF THE NUCLEAR AGE, SURROUNDED BY THE CHAOS OF THE VIETNAM WAR, THE ASSASSINATION OF JOHN F. KENNEDY AND HIS BROTHER, ROBERT KENNEDY, AND FACING THE TUMULT OF A NATION AT MORAL WAR WITH ITSELF, HILLARY EXPLORED BOTH MAJOR AMERICAN POLITICAL PHILOSOPHIES.

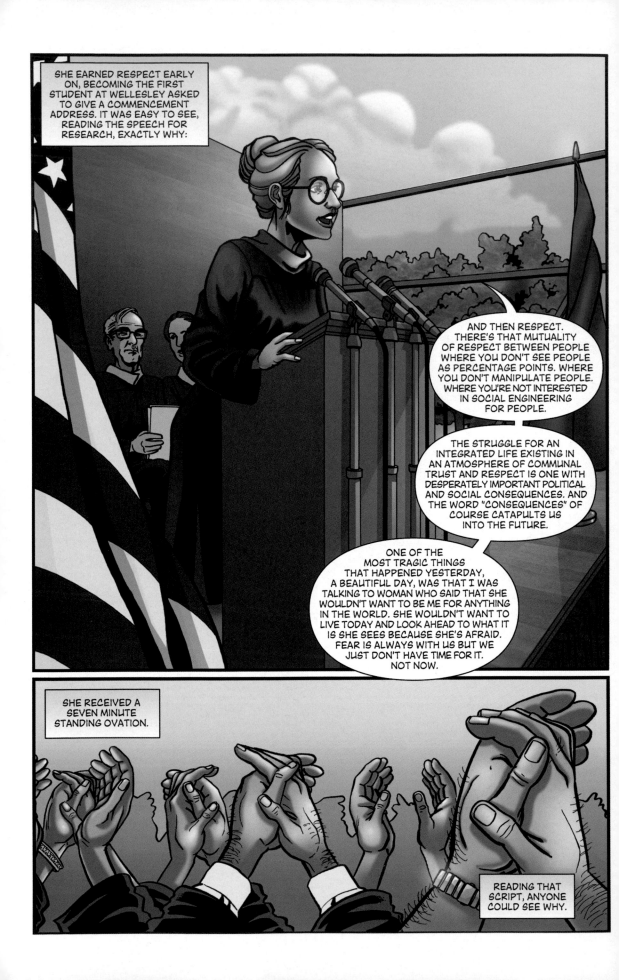

SHE WENT TO YALE AFTER A SUMMER OF SLIMING FISH, A SUMMER IN WHICH SHE NEARLY SHUT DOWN THE CANNERY BY NOTING UNHEALTHY WORKING CONDITIONS.

SHE STUDIED EARLY CHILDHOOD DEVELOPMENT AND WORKED IN THE YALE CHILD STUDY CENTER.

SHE BEGAN DATING A SIGNIFICANTLY HAIRIER BILL CLINTON THAN THE PRESIDENT WE KNOW, AND ALSO BEGAN DEFINING HER SCHOLARLY AMBITION, RELEASING PAPERS ON THE COGNIZANCE OF CHILDREN THAT WERE OFT-CITED AND WELL-REGARDED.

SHE TURNED DOWN BILL'S REQUEST FOR MARRIAGE AT FIRST, ATTENDING TO HER STUDIES AND FOCUSING ON HER CAREER. UNLIKE NOW, THIS WAS HARDLY COMMONPLACE, AND A DECISION THAT FAMILY SPURNED.

WHEN THEY EVENTUALLY MARRIED, SHE KEPT HER MAIDEN NAME, RODHAM, MUCH TO THE CHAGRIN OF BOTH THE MOTHER OF THE BRIDE AND THE MOTHER OF THE GROOM.

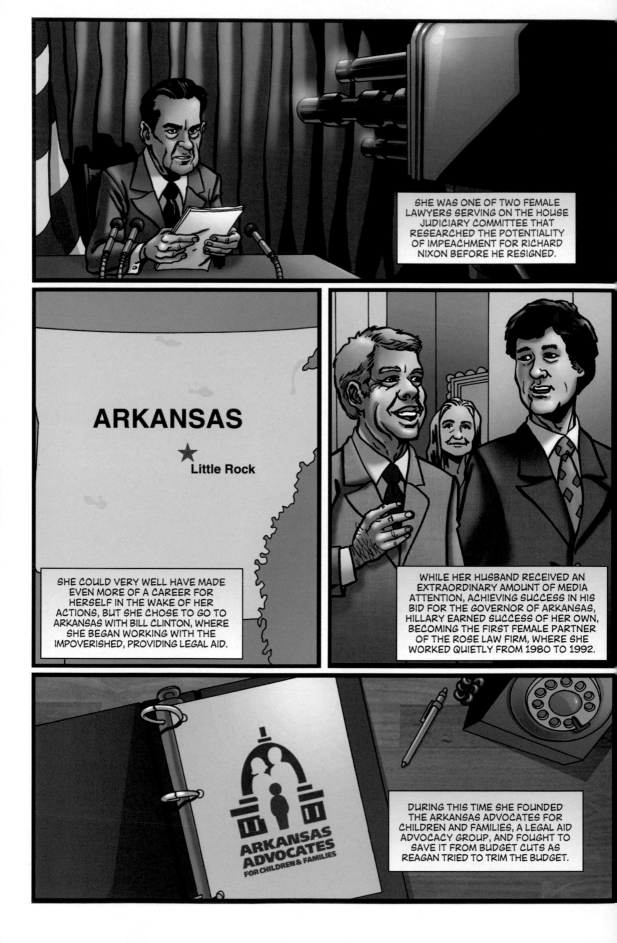

SHE WAS ONE OF TWO FEMALE LAWYERS SERVING ON THE HOUSE JUDICIARY COMMITTEE THAT RESEARCHED THE POTENTIALITY OF IMPEACHMENT FOR RICHARD NIXON BEFORE HE RESIGNED.

ARKANSAS

★

Little Rock

SHE COULD VERY WELL HAVE MADE EVEN MORE OF A CAREER FOR HERSELF IN THE WAKE OF HER ACTIONS, BUT SHE CHOSE TO GO TO ARKANSAS WITH BILL CLINTON, WHERE SHE BEGAN WORKING WITH THE IMPOVERISHED, PROVIDING LEGAL AID.

WHILE HER HUSBAND RECEIVED AN EXTRAORDINARY AMOUNT OF MEDIA ATTENTION, ACHIEVING SUCCESS IN HIS BID FOR THE GOVERNOR OF ARKANSAS, HILLARY EARNED SUCCESS OF HER OWN, BECOMING THE FIRST FEMALE PARTNER OF THE ROSE LAW FIRM, WHERE SHE WORKED QUIETLY FROM 1980 TO 1992.

ARKANSAS ADVOCATES
FOR CHILDREN & FAMILIES

DURING THIS TIME SHE FOUNDED THE ARKANSAS ADVOCATES FOR CHILDREN AND FAMILIES, A LEGAL AID ADVOCACY GROUP, AND FOUGHT TO SAVE IT FROM BUDGET CUTS AS REAGAN TRIED TO TRIM THE BUDGET.

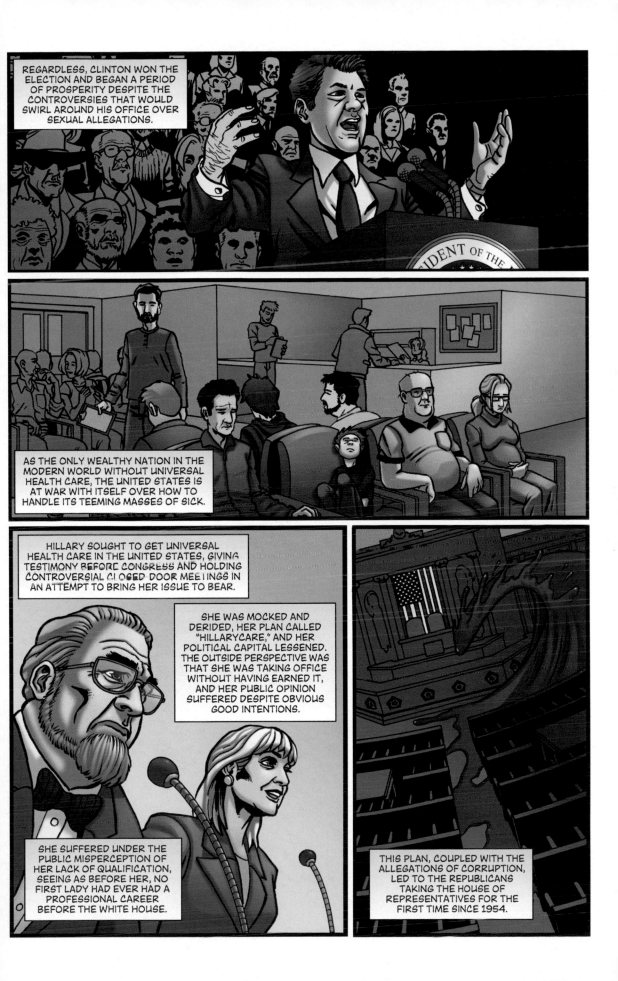

REGARDLESS, CLINTON WON THE ELECTION AND BEGAN A PERIOD OF PROSPERITY DESPITE THE CONTROVERSIES THAT WOULD SWIRL AROUND HIS OFFICE OVER SEXUAL ALLEGATIONS.

AS THE ONLY WEALTHY NATION IN THE MODERN WORLD WITHOUT UNIVERSAL HEALTH CARE, THE UNITED STATES IS AT WAR WITH ITSELF OVER HOW TO HANDLE ITS TEEMING MASSES OF SICK.

HILLARY SOUGHT TO GET UNIVERSAL HEALTH CARE IN THE UNITED STATES, GIVING TESTIMONY BEFORE CONGRESS AND HOLDING CONTROVERSIAL CLOSED-DOOR MEETINGS IN AN ATTEMPT TO BRING HER ISSUE TO BEAR.

SHE WAS MOCKED AND DERIDED, HER PLAN CALLED "HILLARYCARE," AND HER POLITICAL CAPITAL LESSENED. THE OUTSIDE PERSPECTIVE WAS THAT SHE WAS TAKING OFFICE WITHOUT HAVING EARNED IT, AND HER PUBLIC OPINION SUFFERED DESPITE OBVIOUS GOOD INTENTIONS.

SHE SUFFERED UNDER THE PUBLIC MISPERCEPTION OF HER LACK OF QUALIFICATION, SEEING AS BEFORE HER, NO FIRST LADY HAD EVER HAD A PROFESSIONAL CAREER BEFORE THE WHITE HOUSE.

THIS PLAN, COUPLED WITH THE ALLEGATIONS OF CORRUPTION, LED TO THE REPUBLICANS TAKING THE HOUSE OF REPRESENTATIVES FOR THE FIRST TIME SINCE 1954.

AS MUCH AS BILL CLINTON HAS DONE FOR THIS COUNTRY, HIS PRESIDENCY WAS MARRED WITH SCANDALS OF INFIDELITY. THEY UNDERMINED HIS GOOD WORKS IN THE EYES OF MANY AT THE TIME.

IN 1998, THE PRESS, NOTABLY THE DRUDGE REPORT, POUNCED ON THE LEWINSKY SCANDAL, CAUSING THE PRESIDENT TO DECLARE, WITH VEHEMENCE:

I DID... NOT... HAVE... SEXUAL... RELATIONS... WITH... THAT... WOMAN!

BUT HE HAD. HE WAS BROUGHT UP ON PERJURY CHARGES AND PUBLICLY CENSURED.

DESPITE LEAVING OFFICE WITH THE HIGHEST APPROVAL RATING OF ANY PRESIDENT IN POLL HISTORY, HE LEFT IN A WASH OF SCANDAL.

NO BIOGRAPHY I COULD FIND MENTIONS HILLARY'S REACTION TO THIS. NOTHING COVERS THE EMOTIONAL DAMAGE IT MUST HAVE CAUSED. HER GRIEF IN THIS MATTER IS LOST TO HISTORY.

BUT IT MUST BE CONSIDERABLE. IT MADE HER, FOR ONCE, RASH.

THE GREAT STORY HERE FOR ANYBODY WILLING TO FIND IT AND WRITE ABOUT IT AND EXPLAIN IT IS THIS VAST RIGHT-WING CONSPIRACY THAT HAS BEEN CONSPIRING AGAINST MY HUSBAND SINCE THE DAY HE ANNOUNCED FOR PRESIDENT.

SHE CRACKED ONCE IN A MOMENT OF TRUE PRESSURE, AND THE MEDIA ASSAILED HER FOR IT. TEN YEARS LATER, THEY STILL JOKE ABOUT THE "RIGHT-WING CONSPIRACY" COMMENT, FOR AS LITTLE AS IT TRULY MEANT AT THE TIME.

UNDAUNTED, HILLARY SPRUNG BACK IN THE WAKE OF THE SCANDAL AND RAN FOR PUBLIC OFFICE ON HER OWN AS A SENATOR FOR THE STATE OF NEW YORK.

SHE WON, AND HAS MAINTAINED HER SENATE SEAT SINCE 2000.

THE FIRST FIRST LADY EVER TO RUN FOR PUBLIC OFFICE.

THE FIRST FIRST LADY WITH A POST-BACCALAUREATE DEGREE.

THE FIRST FIRST LADY WITH AN OFFICE IN THE WEST WING.

AND AS MENTIONED, THE FIRST FIRST LADY TO HAVE A PROFESSIONAL CAREER BEFORE THE WHITE HOUSE.

MANY, MANY FIRSTS. THERE ISN'T ENOUGH ROOM HERE FOR THEM ALL.

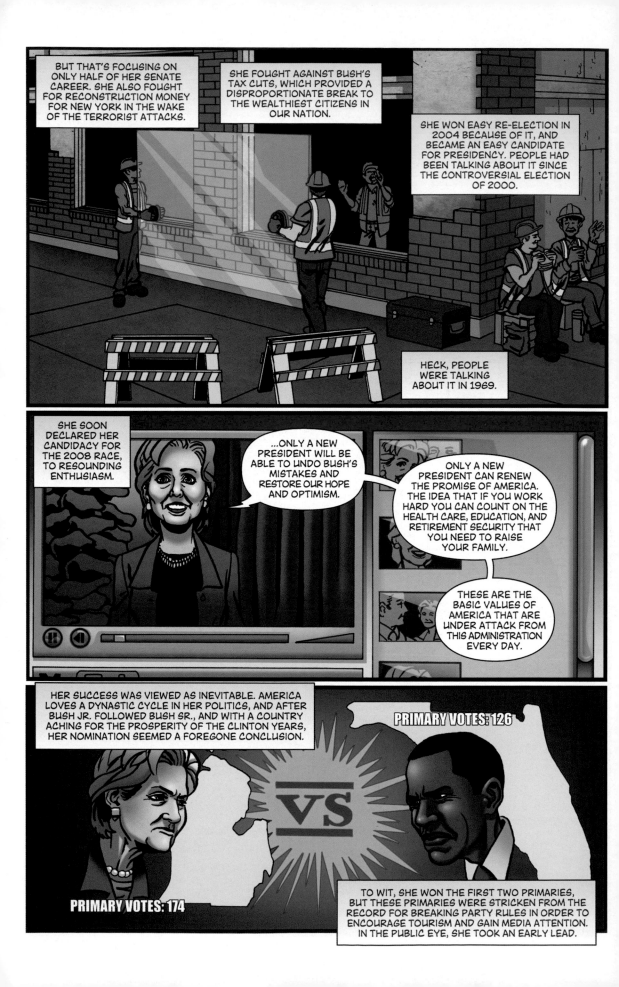

SHE ATTENDED WASILLA HIGH SCHOOL IN THE LATE SEVENTIES AS THE POPULATION OF WASILLA WENT FROM JUST THREE HUNDRED TO APPROXIMATELY FIFTEEN HUNDRED.

AS NUMBER TWENTY-TWO, SARAH "BARRACUDA" HEATH THE POINT GUARD PROVED A LEADER EVEN AT A YOUNG AGE, GIVEN HER STEADFAST DETERMINATION AND COMPETITIVE PLAY.

DESPITE ANKLE INJURIES, SHE PLAYED TO THE END IN THE 1982 CHAMPIONSHIP GAMES, A SPIRITED ATHLETE WHO RAN 10 K RACES WITH HER FAMILY FROM A VERY YOUNG AGE --

-- A TREND THAT CONTINUED THROUGH RECENTLY, WHERE SHE COMPLETED A FOUR HOUR RUN DUBBED "HUMPY'S MARATHON" IN 2005.

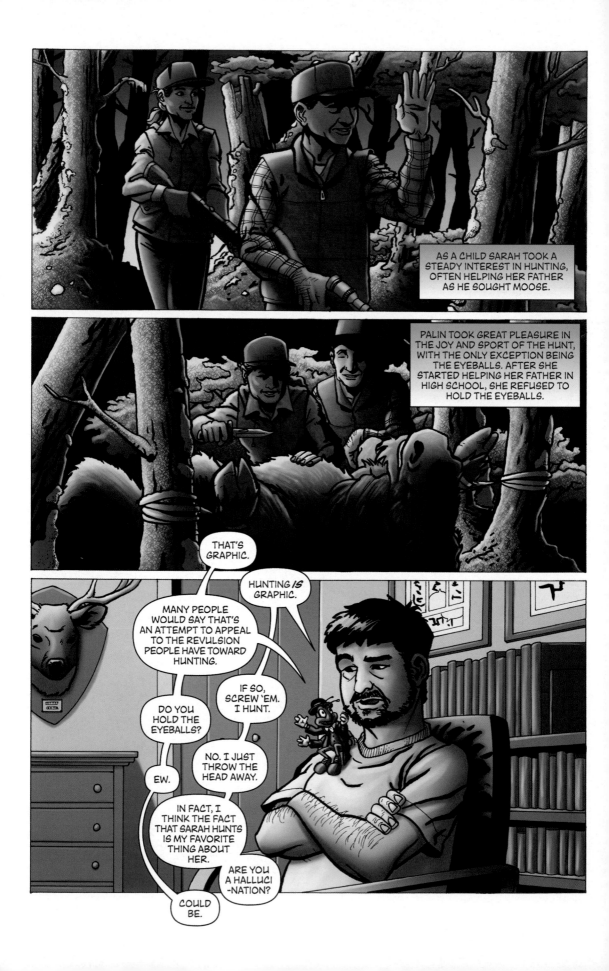

SHE WAS A DEDICATED STUDENT, EARNING A DEGREE IN COMMUNICATIONS/JOURNALISM IN 1987, ATTENDING COLLEGES IN ALASKA, HAWAII, AND IDAHO, THE STATE WHERE SHE ULTIMATELY GRADUATED.

PALIN ASSERTS THAT WHAT DROVE HER INTO POLITICS WAS A CONCERN OVER A SALES TAX ENACTED BY THE LOCAL CITY COUNCIL. TO THAT END, SHE DECIDED TO RUN FOR OFFICE HERSELF, AS A REPUBLICAN.

BALLOT

WASILLA, AK
CITY COUNCIL ELECTION, SEAT E, 199

SARAH PALIN

JOHN HARTRICK

WRITE IN:

PALIN WORKED IN NEWS AS A SPORTS REPORTER FOR THE FRONTIERSMAN, A LOCAL NEWSPAPER, AND ALSO FOR SEVERAL LOCAL TELEVISION STATIONS IN 1988 BEFORE DECIDING TO RUN FOR CITY COUNCIL.

SHE BEAT INCUMBENT JOHN HARTRICK FIVE HUNDRED THIRTY TO THREE HUNDRED TEN, AND WON AGAIN IN 1995 AS THE INCUMBENT.

ACTIVE IN PUBLIC LIFE AS WELL, PALIN'S HUSBAND, TODD PALIN, IS A FOUR TIME WINNER IN THE IRON DOG SNOW RACE, A TWO THOUSAND MILE TREK. TOGETHER, THEY GAINED A SOCIAL VISIBILITY THROUGH THE RACE AND PALIN'S PUBLIC SERVICE.

SPURRED ON BY HER EXPERIENCE AS A CITY COUNCIL MEMBER, PALIN RAN AGAINST THE INCUMBENT THREE TIME MAYOR OF HER CITY, WINNING THE ELECTION BY TWO HUNDRED VOTES IN AN ELECTION WHERE APPROXIMATELY ELEVEN HUNDRED PEOPLE WENT TO THE POLLS.

WASILLA CITY HALL

SHE IMMEDIATELY MOVED TO CUT SPENDING AND BRING ACCOUNTABILITY TO THE LOCAL GOVERNMENT, SPURRING CONTROVERSY AND GAINING FOLLOWERS.

SHE DISMISSED THE MUSEUM DIRECTOR, AND ASKED FOR RESIGNATIONS FROM THE POLICE CHIEF, THE LIBRARIAN, AND THE PUBLIC WORKS DIRECTOR.

NOT TO EXCLUDER HERSELF FROM HER CULLING OF GRAFT, SHE FULFILLED A CAMPAIGN PROMISE AND CUT HER OWN SALARY BY TEN PERCENT, A CHANGE THE CITY COUNCIL LATER NULLIFIED.

NOW AT THE CENTER OF LOCAL CONTROVERSY, UNDOUBTEDLY SARAH WAS WORKING HARD TO ENACT HER VISION OF GOVERNMENT ON A LOCAL LEVEL.

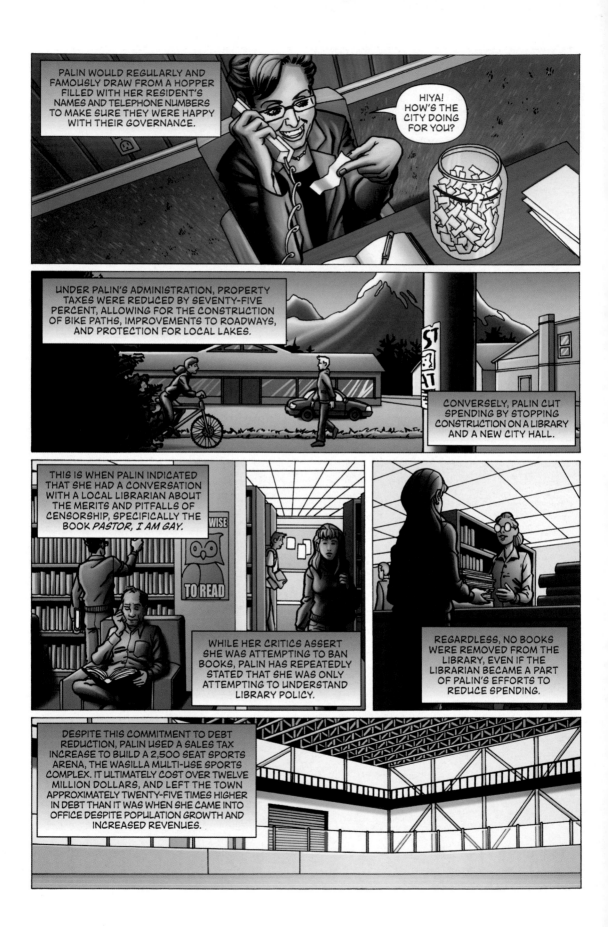

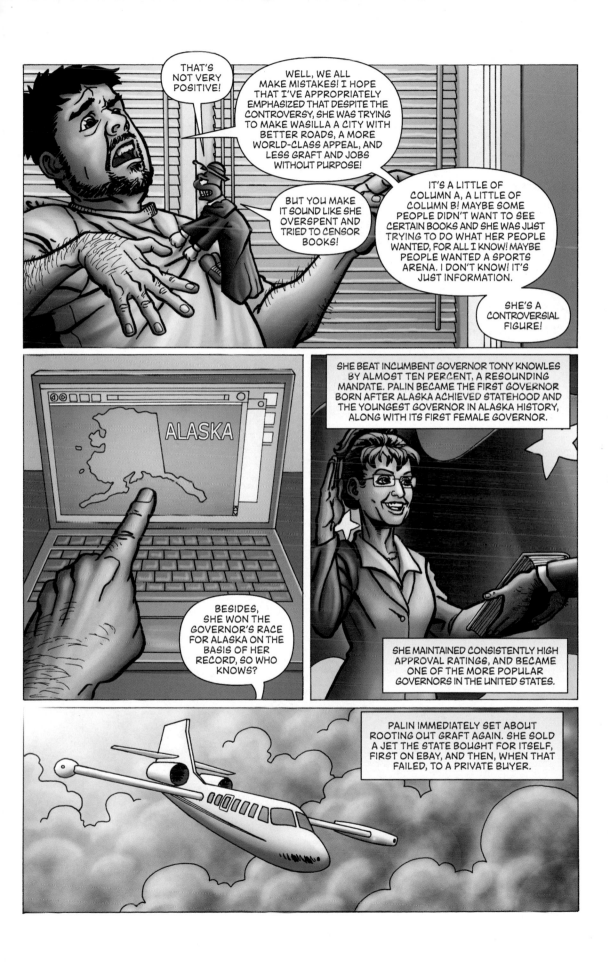

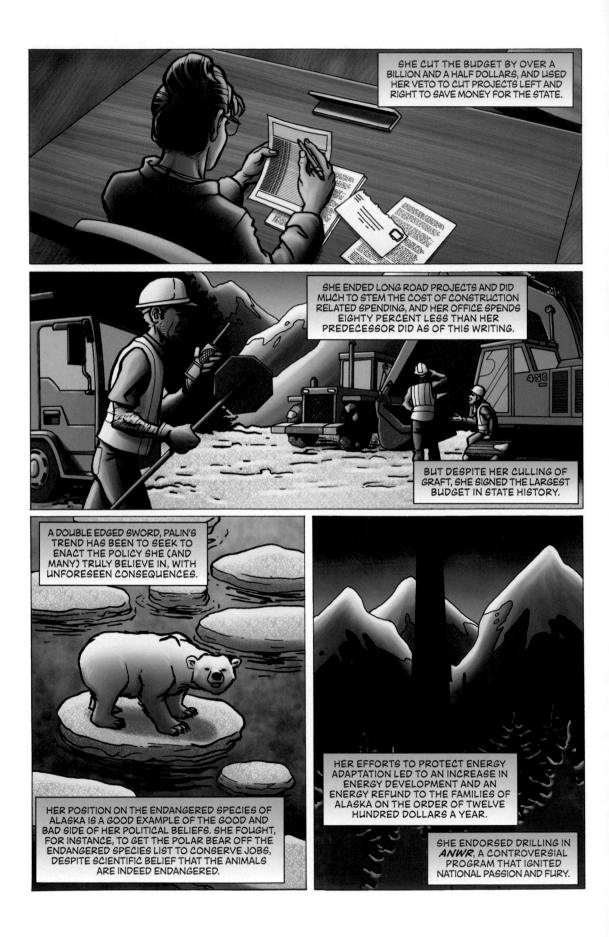

SHE CUT THE BUDGET BY OVER A BILLION AND A HALF DOLLARS, AND USED HER VETO TO CUT PROJECTS LEFT AND RIGHT TO SAVE MONEY FOR THE STATE.

SHE ENDED LONG ROAD PROJECTS AND DID MUCH TO STEM THE COST OF CONSTRUCTION RELATED SPENDING, AND HER OFFICE SPENDS EIGHTY PERCENT LESS THAN HER PREDECESSOR DID AS OF THIS WRITING.

BUT DESPITE HER CULLING OF GRAFT, SHE SIGNED THE LARGEST BUDGET IN STATE HISTORY.

A DOUBLE EDGED SWORD, PALIN'S TREND HAS BEEN TO SEEK TO ENACT THE POLICY SHE (AND MANY) TRULY BELIEVE IN, WITH UNFORESEEN CONSEQUENCES.

HER POSITION ON THE ENDANGERED SPECIES OF ALASKA IS A GOOD EXAMPLE OF THE GOOD AND BAD SIDE OF HER POLITICAL BELIEFS. SHE FOUGHT, FOR INSTANCE, TO GET THE POLAR BEAR OFF THE ENDANGERED SPECIES LIST TO CONSERVE JOBS, DESPITE SCIENTIFIC BELIEF THAT THE ANIMALS ARE INDEED ENDANGERED.

HER EFFORTS TO PROTECT ENERGY ADAPTATION LED TO AN INCREASE IN ENERGY DEVELOPMENT AND AN ENERGY REFUND TO THE FAMILIES OF ALASKA ON THE ORDER OF TWELVE HUNDRED DOLLARS A YEAR.

SHE ENDORSED DRILLING IN *ANWR*, A CONTROVERSIAL PROGRAM THAT IGNITED NATIONAL PASSION AND FURY.

AND THEN THERE'S "TROOPERGATE."

AFTER A STATE TROOPER, MIKE WOOTEN, WAS NOT FIRED AT PALIN'S REQUEST, PALIN DISMISSED THE TROOPER'S SUPERVISOR, WALTER MONEGAN.

IT TURNS OUT THAT THE MOTIVATION FOR THE DISMISSAL WAS WOOTEN'S CUSTODY BATTLE WITH PALIN'S SISTER, WHO THE TROOPER HAD RECENTLY DIVORCED.

DESPITE BEING A REPUBLICAN ORGANIZATION, THE ALASKAN LEGISLATIVE COUNCIL INDICATED THAT PALIN HAD ABUSED HER POWER, AND RELEASED A REPORT INDICATING AS MUCH AS PALIN BEGAN HER RUN FOR VICE PRESIDENT.

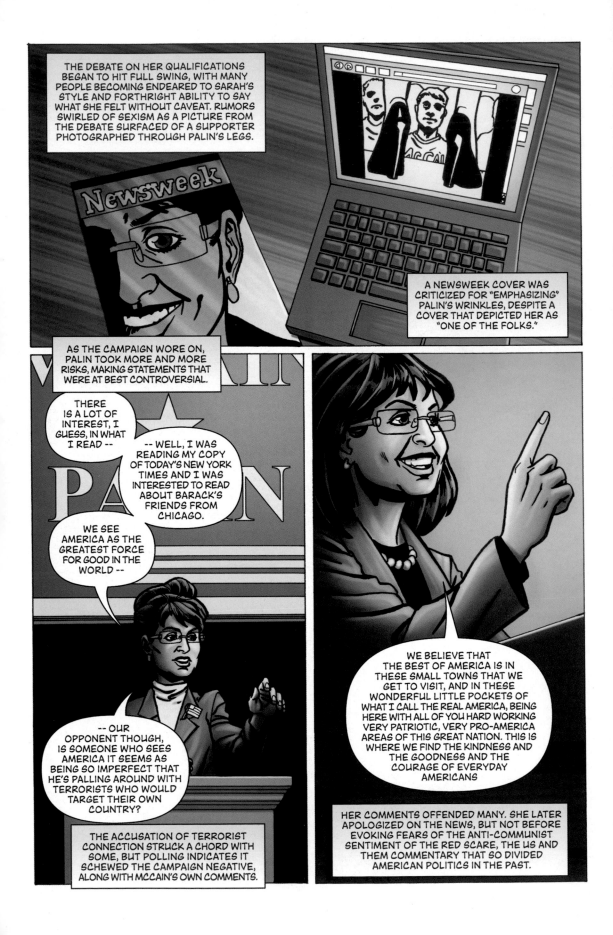

THE DEBATE ON HER QUALIFICATIONS BEGAN TO HIT FULL SWING, WITH MANY PEOPLE BECOMING ENDEARED TO SARAH'S STYLE AND FORTHRIGHT ABILITY TO SAY WHAT SHE FELT WITHOUT CAVEAT. RUMORS SWIRLED OF SEXISM AS A PICTURE FROM THE DEBATE SURFACED OF A SUPPORTER PHOTOGRAPHED THROUGH PALIN'S LEGS.

A NEWSWEEK COVER WAS CRITICIZED FOR "EMPHASIZING" PALIN'S WRINKLES, DESPITE A COVER THAT DEPICTED HER AS "ONE OF THE FOLKS."

AS THE CAMPAIGN WORE ON, PALIN TOOK MORE AND MORE RISKS, MAKING STATEMENTS THAT WERE AT BEST CONTROVERSIAL.

THERE IS A LOT OF INTEREST, I GUESS, IN WHAT I READ --

-- WELL, I WAS READING MY COPY OF TODAY'S NEW YORK TIMES AND I WAS INTERESTED TO READ ABOUT BARACK'S FRIENDS FROM CHICAGO.

WE SEE AMERICA AS THE GREATEST FORCE FOR GOOD IN THE WORLD --

-- OUR OPPONENT THOUGH, IS SOMEONE WHO SEES AMERICA IT SEEMS AS BEING SO IMPERFECT THAT HE'S PALLING AROUND WITH TERRORISTS WHO WOULD TARGET THEIR OWN COUNTRY?

THE ACCUSATION OF TERRORIST CONNECTION STRUCK A CHORD WITH SOME, BUT POLLING INDICATES IT SCHEWED THE CAMPAIGN NEGATIVE, ALONG WITH MCCAIN'S OWN COMMENTS.

WE BELIEVE THAT THE BEST OF AMERICA IS IN THESE SMALL TOWNS THAT WE GET TO VISIT, AND IN THESE WONDERFUL LITTLE POCKETS OF WHAT I CALL THE REAL AMERICA, BEING HERE WITH ALL OF YOU HARD WORKING VERY PATRIOTIC, VERY PRO-AMERICA AREAS OF THIS GREAT NATION. THIS IS WHERE WE FIND THE KINDNESS AND THE GOODNESS AND THE COURAGE OF EVERYDAY AMERICANS

HER COMMENTS OFFENDED MANY. SHE LATER APOLOGIZED ON THE NEWS, BUT NOT BEFORE EVOKING FEARS OF THE ANTI-COMMUNIST SENTIMENT OF THE RED SCARE, THE US AND THEM COMMENTARY THAT SO DIVIDED AMERICAN POLITICS IN THE PAST.

CONTROVERSY AROSE WHEN NEWS REPORTS INDICATED THAT THE GOP SPENT UPWARDS OF ONE HUNDRED FIFTY THOUSAND DOLLARS CLOTHING PALIN FOR THE CAMPAIGN.

PALIN BECAME A GRANDMOTHER IN THE DECEMBER FOLLOWING THE ELECTION, RAISING ISSUES OF MOTHERHOOD AND FAMILY VALUES.

ON ONE HAND, PALIN ADMONISHED HER DAUGHTER TO AVOID AN ABORTION DESPITE A TEENAGE PREGNANCY.

BRISTOL'S FUTURE MOTHER-IN-LAW PLEADS
NOT GUILTY

ON THE OTHER HAND, BRISTOL, THE DAUGHTER IN QUESTION, IS NOW A MOTHER AT A VERY EARLY AGE COPING WITH UNTOLD PRESSURES, WITH HER FUTURE MOTHER-IN-LAW ACCUSED OF DRUG DEALING, HER FACE ACROSS NEWSPAPERS, AND HER LIFE UNDER A MICROSCOPE.

CAROLINE KENNEDY WAS BORN ON NOVEMBER 27TH, 1957.

SHE WAS NAMED AFTER HER MATERNAL AUNT.

SHE WAS BORN INTO THE CLOSEST THING AMERICAN HAS TO A MULTI-GENERATIONAL DYNASTY. HER FAMILY WAS SO IMPORTANT TO SOCIETY, WHETHER YOU LIKE THEM OR LOATHE THEM, THAT WE CRAFTED AN ENTIRE SOCIAL FEELING AROUND THEM WITH ONE WORD.

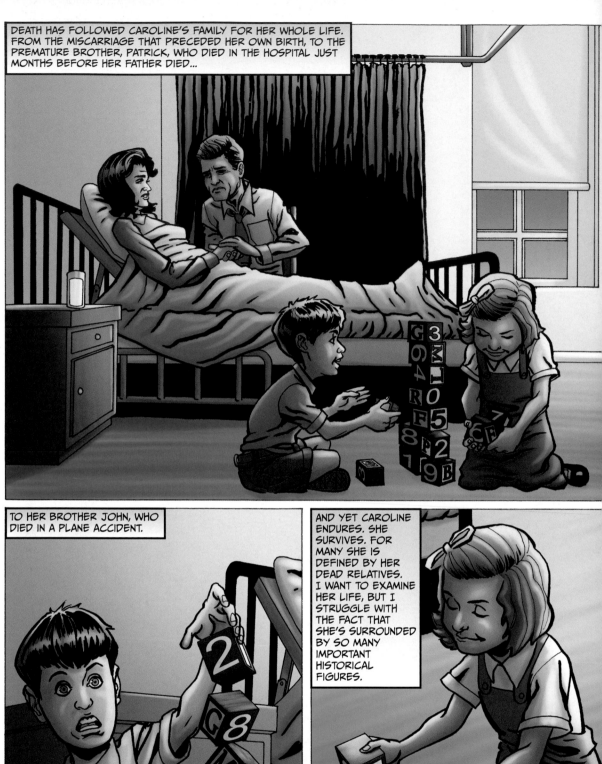

DEATH HAS FOLLOWED CAROLINE'S FAMILY FOR HER WHOLE LIFE. FROM THE MISCARRIAGE THAT PRECEDED HER OWN BIRTH, TO THE PREMATURE BROTHER, PATRICK, WHO DIED IN THE HOSPITAL JUST MONTHS BEFORE HER FATHER DIED...

TO HER BROTHER JOHN, WHO DIED IN A PLANE ACCIDENT.

AND YET CAROLINE ENDURES. SHE SURVIVES. FOR MANY SHE IS DEFINED BY HER DEAD RELATIVES. I WANT TO EXAMINE HER LIFE, BUT I STRUGGLE WITH THE FACT THAT SHE'S SURROUNDED BY SO MANY IMPORTANT HISTORICAL FIGURES.

I'M SURE SHE DOES, TOO.

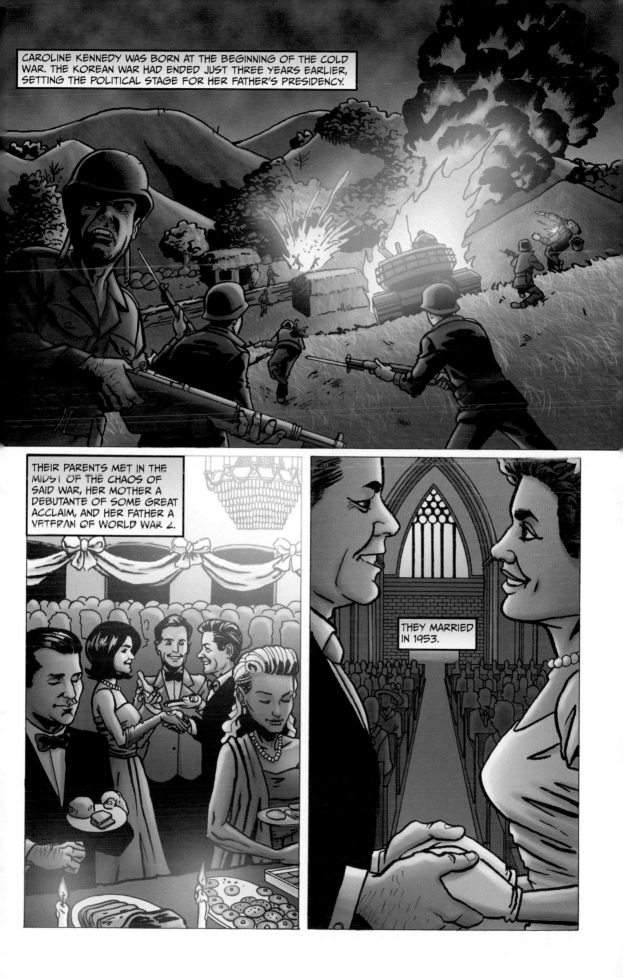

CAROLINE KENNEDY WAS BORN AT THE BEGINNING OF THE COLD WAR. THE KOREAN WAR HAD ENDED JUST THREE YEARS EARLIER, SETTING THE POLITICAL STAGE FOR HER FATHER'S PRESIDENCY.

THEIR PARENTS MET IN THE MIDST OF THE CHAOS OF SAID WAR, HER MOTHER A DEBUTANTE OF SOME GREAT ACCLAIM, AND HER FATHER A VETERAN OF WORLD WAR 2.

THEY MARRIED IN 1953.

CAROLINE WAS A CHILD BORN INTO A WEALTHY FAMILY. DESPITE THE TRAGEDIES THAT LATER BEFELL HER, SHE KNEW MANY COMFORTS, LIKE HER PONY, MACARONI.

SHE WAS AN INTELLIGENT AND SOMETIMES SHY CHILD. IN THE FAMOUS SHOT WHERE JOHN-JOHN SALUTES HIS FATHER, SHE IS NOTABLY QUIET, AS IF THE PERFORMANCE OF CELEBRITY DISINTERESTED HER.

THIS SPIRIT, DISPLAYED EVEN AT SUCH A YOUNG AGE, LED NEIL DIAMOND TO WRITE HIS SONG "SWEET CAROLINE" IN HER HONOR.

HER FIRST WORDS WERE "PLANE," "GOODBYE," AND "NEW HAMPSHIRE."

WHEN HER FATHER WAS MURDERED, CAROLINE WAS INFORMED BY THE NANNY, MAUD SHAW, AGAINST THE WISHES OF HER MOTHER, JACQUELINE.

IT CAUSED A RIFT BETWEEN JACKIE AND MAUD, BUT IN MY EYES IT SHOWS A BIT OF THE CLINICAL DISASSOCIATION BETWEEN THE REAL PERSON AND THE THINGS HAPPENING IN THEIR LIVES WHEN WEALTH AND POWER ENTER THE PICTURE. IT CHANGES PEOPLE.

WHEN CAROLINE'S MOTHER REMARRIED A MAN NAMED ARISTOTLE ONASSIS, CAROLINE FACED WHAT TO SOME MIGHT SEEM THE DAUNTING PROCESS OF RECEDING FROM THE SPOTLIGHT AT THE AGE OF ELEVEN FOR HER OWN PROTECTION.

I WOULD SPECULATE SHE'D HAVE SEEN IT AS A BLESSING.

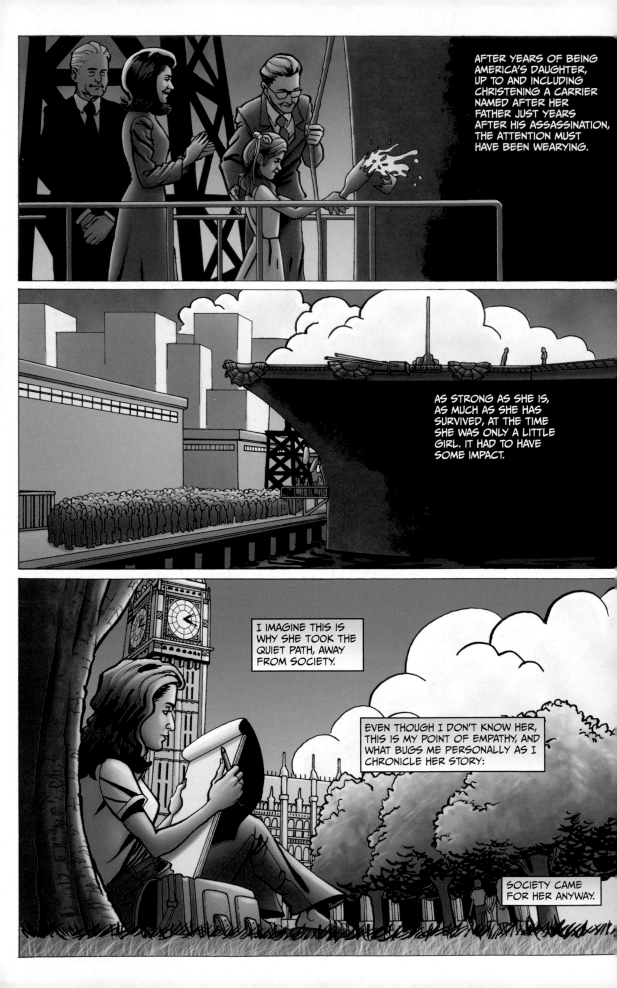

IN 1975, AS SHE REACHED ADULTHOOD, A CATASTROPHIC CAR BOMB ATTACK FROM THE IRA AIMED AT HER HOST IN LONDON NEARLY KILLED HER. SHE WAS ONLY SAVED BY HER OWN TARDINESS.

SHE INTERNED FOR THE DAILY NEWS, MOVING FROM THE SUBJECT OF CURIOSITY TO SOMEONE WHOSE JOB IT WAS TO FETCH THE COFFEE.

ON THE ONE HAND, SHE WAS CHANGING TYPEWRITING RIBBONS FOR REPORTERS.

ON THE OTHER HAND, SHE WAS COMMISSIONED BY ROLLING STONE TO WRITE ABOUT THE DEATH OF ELVIS PRESLEY, SO SHE COULD HARDLY BE CALLED A LOWLY LACKEY ON THE BOTTOM RUNG, THOUGH I'M SURE THE DIFFERENCE IN TREATMENT MUST HAVE BEEN CONFUSING.

IT SEEMS CRUEL TO ME TO SEND THE DAUGHTER OF ONE SLAIN KING TO COVER THE DEATH OF ANOTHER. BUT IT ALSO SEEMS SURPRISINGLY APT.

SHE'S RICH, BUT SHE'S BEEN PUT IN LOWLY POSITIONS. SHE'S SHIED FROM ATTENTION, AND YET ALWAYS SEEMS AT THE CENTER OF IT.

CAROLINE GRADUATED FROM RADCLIFFE (NOW ASSIMILATED INTO HARVARD) IN 1979, AND SOON TOOK A POSITION AT THE METROPOLITAN MUSEUM OF ART AFTER BRIEFLY INTERNING WITH TED KENNEDY.

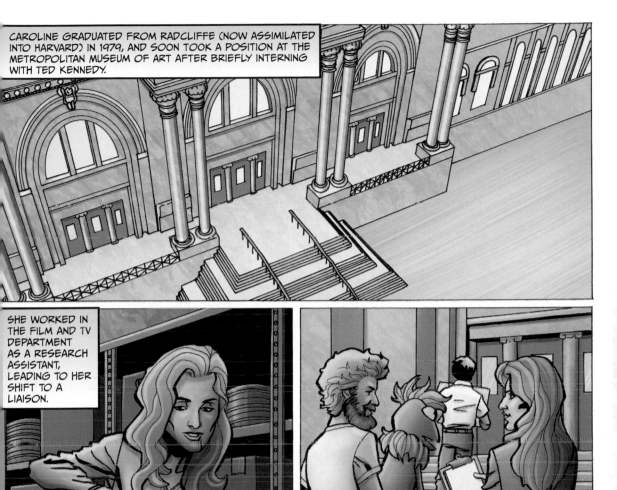

SHE WORKED IN THE FILM AND TV DEPARTMENT AS A RESEARCH ASSISTANT, LEADING TO HER SHIFT TO A LIAISON.

IF YOU'RE A RIGHTEOUSLY OLD NERD LIKE ME BUT YOUR MEMORY IS STILL INTACT, YOU MIGHT REMEMBER THE *DON'T EAT THE PICTURES* SESAME STREET SPECIAL. SHE HELPED COORDINATE THE FILMING AT THE MUSEUM.

WHILE THERE SHE MET *EDWIN SCHLOSSBERG.*

THE PAIR WERE MARRIED IN 1986, IN A CEREMONY THAT MADE HEADLINES.

CONTRARY TO FAULTY REPORTING, SHE KEPT HER NAME, AND WAS NEVER CAROLINE KENNEDY SCHLOSSBERG.

IN 1988, SHE GRADUATED FROM COLUMBIA LAW SCHOOL AT THE TOP END OF HER CLASS.

WITHIN THE YEAR HER FIRST CHILD ROSE WAS BORN.

ROSE WAS NAMED AFTER CAROLINE'S GRANDMOTHER, JOHN F. KENNEDY'S MOTHER, THE LONGEST LIVING PRESIDENTIAL RELATIVE AND A FIGURE OF MUCH PROMINENCE IN HER DAY.

CAROLINE HAD THREE CHILDREN OVER THE COURSE OF THE LATE EIGHTIES AND EARLY NINETIES.

THE FAMILY IS NOT VERY PROMINENT IN THE MEDIA, PERHAPS DUE TO JACKIE KENNEDY'S INFLUENCE AND PROTECTION, WHICH DROVE HER CHILDREN TO BE HAPPY AND HEALTHY.

AND YEAH, THERE ARE SOME POTENTIAL TABLOID STORIES ABOUT THE KIDS. BUT YOU KNOW WHAT?

MOON ME

THEY'RE NOT PERTINENT. SO IF YOU WANT TO HEAR ABOUT THESE KIDS, WAIT UNTIL THEY'RE BRILLIANT MEMBERS OF SOCIETY.

THEN WE'LL WRITE THEIR BIOGRAPHY. I'M NOT GONNA DIG ON KIDS. BESIDES, THEY'LL UNDOUBTEDLY HAVE THEIR OWN BIOGRAPHIES.

MOON M

CAROLINE'S BROTHER, JOHN KENNEDY, DIED IN 1999 AFTER HIS SMALL PLANE CRASHED IN POOR WEATHER CONDITIONS.

I'M LOATHE TO MENTION IT, BECAUSE IT'S PART OF THE STRANGE CULT OF INFORMATION SURROUNDING HER FAMILY'S PROXIMITY TO DEATH.

I WILL MENTION IT, HOWEVER, BECAUSE IT'S IMPORTANT TO NOTE THAT JOHN WAS A LARGE PART OF HER LIFE, AND HIS DEATH MUST HAVE IMPACTED HER TERRIBLY.

NO MATTER HOW MUCH SHE DISTINGUISHES HERSELF, SHE SEEMS TO BE DEFINED IN THE MEDIA BY THE LOSSES IN HER LIFE, NOT THE GAINS SHE'S MADE IN LIFE.

I HOPE I'M NOT HELPING THAT, BUT IT'S SO PROMINENT.

HE WAS THE ONLY PERSON LIVING WHO HAD ALSO EXPERIENCED THE HIGHS OF WEALTH AND THE DEPTHS OF TRAGEDY THE FAMILY IS KNOWN FOR. NOW SHE REMAINS AS THE LONE LEGACY, IN THAT RESPECT.

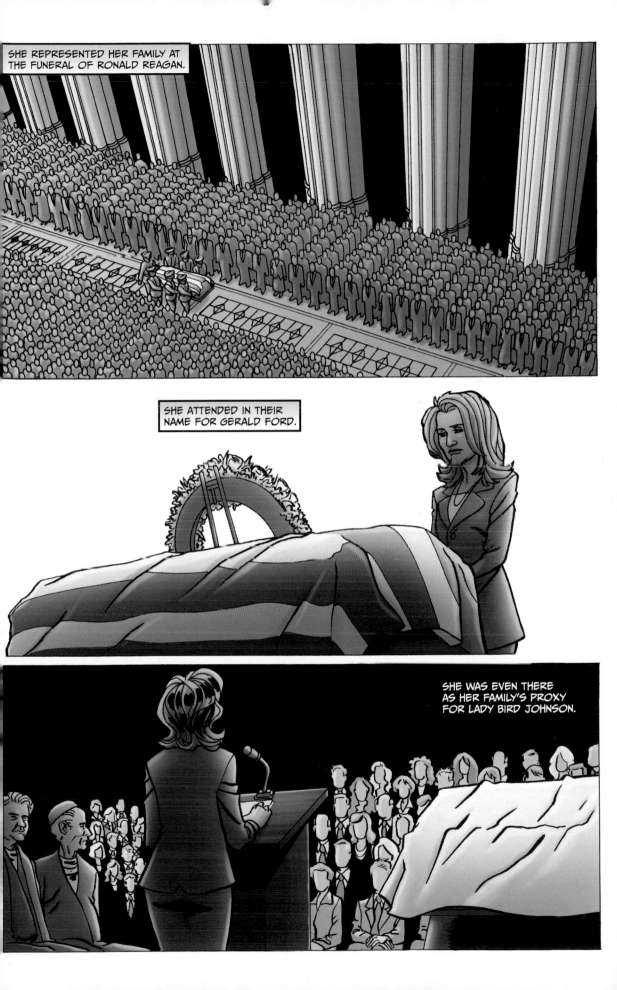

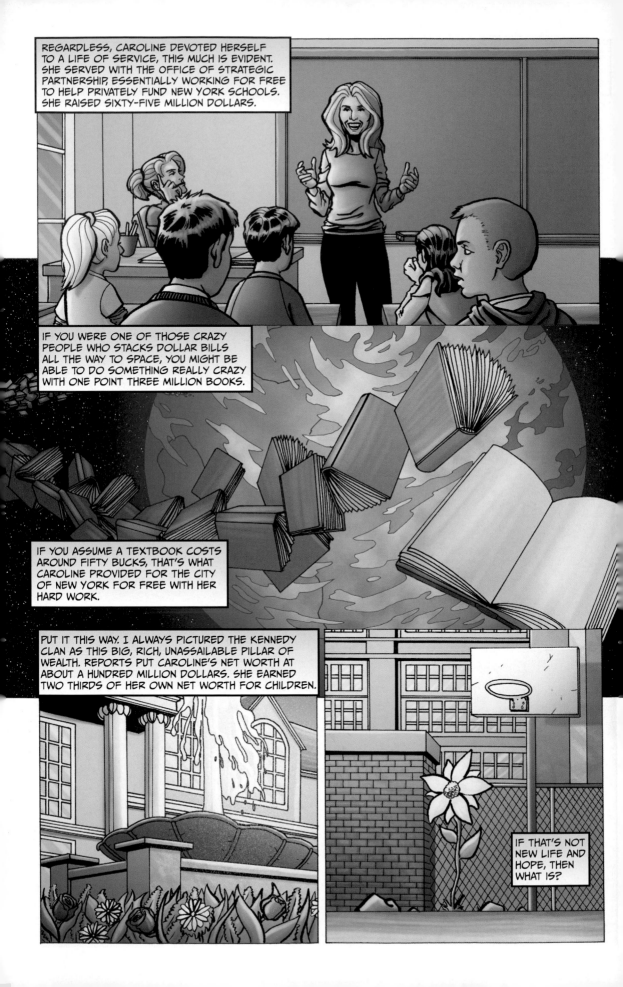

REGARDLESS, CAROLINE DEVOTED HERSELF TO A LIFE OF SERVICE, THIS MUCH IS EVIDENT. SHE SERVED WITH THE OFFICE OF STRATEGIC PARTNERSHIP, ESSENTIALLY WORKING FOR FREE TO HELP PRIVATELY FUND NEW YORK SCHOOLS. SHE RAISED SIXTY-FIVE MILLION DOLLARS.

IF YOU WERE ONE OF THOSE CRAZY PEOPLE WHO STACKS DOLLAR BILLS ALL THE WAY TO SPACE, YOU MIGHT BE ABLE TO DO SOMETHING REALLY CRAZY WITH ONE POINT THREE MILLION BOOKS.

IF YOU ASSUME A TEXTBOOK COSTS AROUND FIFTY BUCKS, THAT'S WHAT CAROLINE PROVIDED FOR THE CITY OF NEW YORK FOR FREE WITH HER HARD WORK.

PUT IT THIS WAY. I ALWAYS PICTURED THE KENNEDY CLAN AS THIS BIG, RICH, UNASSAILABLE PILLAR OF WEALTH. REPORTS PUT CAROLINE'S NET WORTH AT ABOUT A HUNDRED MILLION DOLLARS. SHE EARNED TWO THIRDS OF HER OWN NET WORTH FOR CHILDREN.

IF THAT'S NOT NEW LIFE AND HOPE, THEN WHAT IS?

IN 2008, WHEN BARACK OBAMA BEGAN RUNNING FOR PRESIDENT, RUMORS BEGAN TO SWIRL AS TO WHETHER OR NOT CAROLINE WOULD ENDORSE HIM.

THE LAST TIME SHE ENDORSED A PRESIDENT WAS TED KENNEDY, BACK IN 1980. PEOPLE WANTED TO KNOW WHAT SHE THOUGHT OF ONE OF THE FIRST MEN SINCE HER FATHER WHO COULD SPARK HOPE IN THE AMERICAN MIND.

GIVEN HER MEDIA PROMINENCE (DESIRED OR UNDESIRED), HER WORD HAS A GREAT VALUE TO AN AMERICA THAT LARGELY VIEWS HER FATHER'S POLITICAL LEGACY AS POSITIVE IN AN ERA OF CYNICISM AND PERIL.

ULTIMATELY, SHE DECIDED TO ENDORSE OBAMA, WHICH HELPED HIS ELECTION CAMPAIGN GAIN THE CREDIBILITY IT NEEDED FOR HIS SUCCESS.

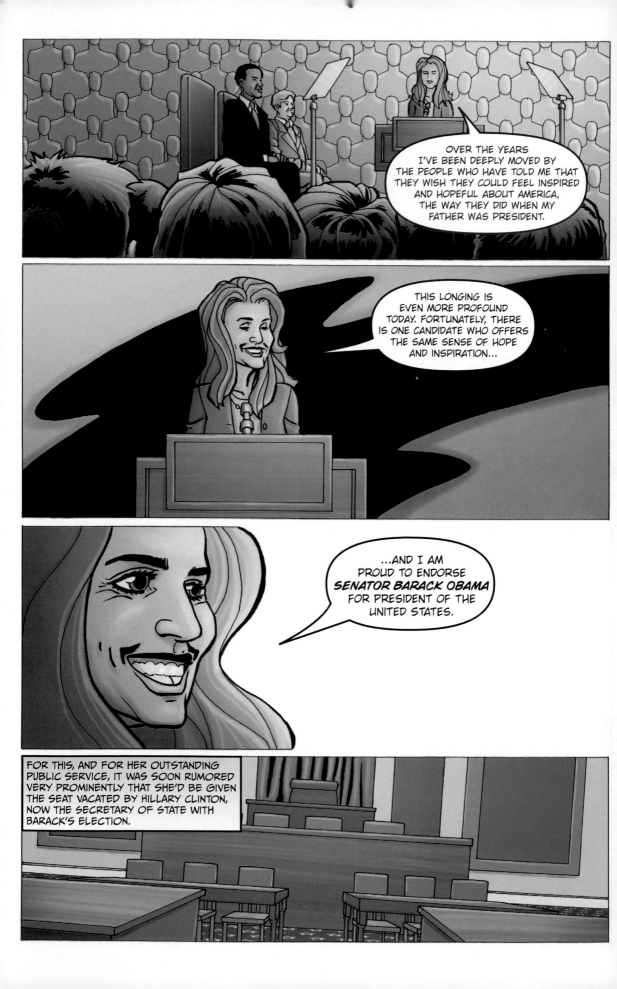

THE PUNDITS FOUGHT, AND MADE HAY OF THE NEWS. IT WAS AS IF THE POSITION HAD ALREADY BEEN OFFERED.

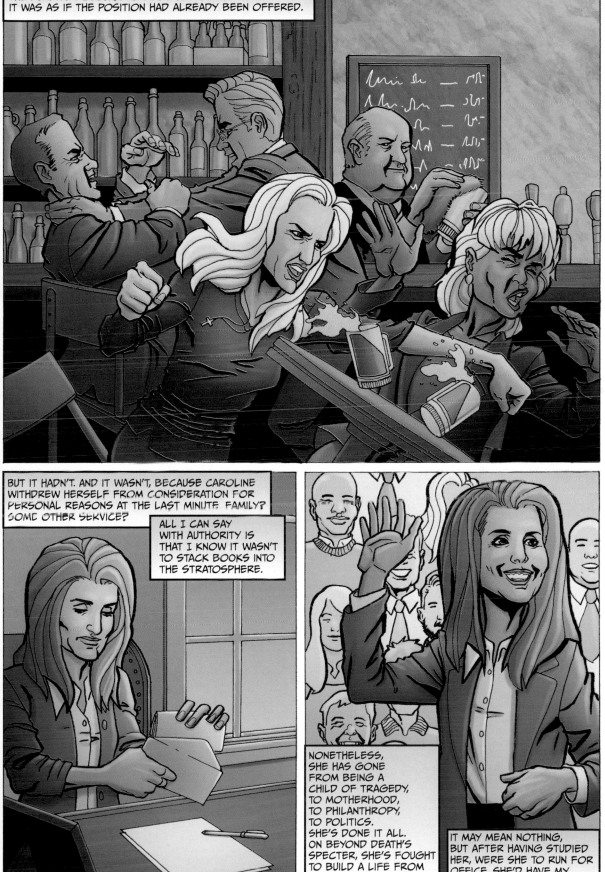

BUT IT HADN'T. AND IT WASN'T, BECAUSE CAROLINE WITHDREW HERSELF FROM CONSIDERATION FOR PERSONAL REASONS AT THE LAST MINUTE. FAMILY? SOME OTHER SERVICE?

ALL I CAN SAY WITH AUTHORITY IS THAT I KNOW IT WASN'T TO STACK BOOKS INTO THE STRATOSPHERE.

NONETHELESS, SHE HAS GONE FROM BEING A CHILD OF TRAGEDY, TO MOTHERHOOD, TO PHILANTHROPY, TO POLITICS. SHE'S DONE IT ALL. ON BEYOND DEATH'S SPECTER, SHE'S FOUGHT TO BUILD A LIFE FROM ASHES, AND SUCCEEDED.

IT MAY MEAN NOTHING, BUT AFTER HAVING STUDIED HER, WERE SHE TO RUN FOR OFFICE, SHE'D HAVE MY ENDORSEMENT.

BIBLIOGRAPHIES

MICHELLE OBAMA

TEXTS:

Michelle by Liza Mundy, Simon & Schuster, 2008

Newsweek, Dec 1, 2008, "What Michelle Means to Us" (Allison Samuels)

"Princeton-Educated Blacks and the Black Community"
(Michelle Obama, Princeton, 1985)
http://www.politico.com/news/stories/0208/8642.html

VIDEO VISUAL/SPEECH REFERENCE:

Obama projected wins: http://www.youtube.com/watch?v=YEmMV2jf6Iw

Jesse Jackson cries: http://www.youtube.com/watch?v=K_IFzZkki44

Obama acceptance speech:
http://www.youtube.com/watch?v=C-ZyqnBVbVE
http://www.youtube.com/watch?v=NtTlepiBQPQ

O'Reilly on lynch party: http://www.youtube.com/watch?v=a1sPIGfpAiE

McCain "Bomb Iran": http://www.youtube.com/watch?v=o-zoPgv_nYg

"Do the Right Thing" ending: http://www.youtube.com/watch?v=fojkVfh0WQI

DNC 2004: http://www.youtube.com/watch?v=eWynt87PaJ0

GENERAL INTERNET REFERENCE:

Newsweek: Barack's Rock: http://www.newsweek.com/id/112849/page/1

Bullet proof glass:
http://blogs.telegraph.co.uk/toby_harnden/blog/2008/11/04/barack_obama_election_
night_speech_to_be_behind_bullet_proof_glass

Slaves and the White House:
http://www.whitehousehistory.org/06/subs/06_a04.html
http://seattletimes.nwsource.com/html/politics/2008466925_obamaslavery04.html

Scottsboro Boys:
http://www.law.umkc.edu/faculty/projects/Ftrials/scottsboro/scottsb.htm

Carl A. Fields Center:
http://www.princeton.edu/~twc/
http://findarticles.com/p/articles/mi_m0DXK/is_7_19/ai_87414506
http://etcweb.princeton.edu/CampusWWW/Companion/third_world_center.html
http://www.princeton.edu/pr/news/02/q2/0415-TWCname.htm

Liza Mundy on Michelle for Democracy Now!:
http://www.democracynow.org/2008/11/13/michelle_obamas_biographer_on_the_
nations

Barack at Harvard:
http://www.boston.com/news/local/articles/2007/01/28/at_harvard_law_a_unifying_
voice/

Michelle and Barney:
http://michelleobamawatch.com/michelle-obama-represented barney-the-dinosaur

Washington Post on Barack and Michelle:
http://www.washingtonpost.com/wp-dyn/content/story/2008/10/03/
ST2008100302144.html?sid=ST2008100302144

"Proud of My Country": http://www.foxnews.com/politics/elections/2008/02/19/
michelle-obama-takes-heat-for-saying-shes-proud-of-my-country-for-the-first-time/

Mayor Daley: http://morsehellhole.blogspot.com/2008/04/daley-shoot-to-kill.html

Michelle's Working Class Credentials examined:
http://www.dailymail.co.uk/femail/article-517824/Mrs-O-The-truth-Michelle-Obamas-
working-class-credentials.html

WIKIPEDIA:

Michelle Obama: http://en.wikipedia.org/wiki/Michelle_Obama

Barack Obama: http://en.wikipedia.org/wiki/Barack_Obama

Jeremiah Wright: http://en.wikipedia.org/wiki/Jeremiah_Wright

Salutorian: http://en.wikipedia.org/wiki/Salutatorian

The Scottsboro Boys: http://en.wikipedia.org/wiki/Scottsboro_Boys

Old Boy Network: http://en.wikipedia.org/wiki/Old_boy_network

Craig Robinson: http://en.wikipedia.org/wiki/Craig_Robinson_(basketball_coach)

Robert Bork: http://en.wikipedia.org/wiki/Robert_Bork

Iran-Contra: http://en.wikipedia.org/wiki/Iran-Contra_affair

Chicago: http://en.wikipedia.org/wiki/Chicago

Chicago's South Side: http://en.wikipedia.org/wiki/South_Side_(Chicago)

Daley 1: http://en.wikipedia.org/wiki/Richard_J._Daley

Daley 2: http://en.wikipedia.org/wiki/Richard_M._Daley

Princeton: http://en.wikipedia.org/wiki/History_of_Princeton_University

Civil Rights Act: http://en.wikipedia.org/wiki/Civil_Rights_Act_of_1964

SELECTED VISUAL REFERENCE:

http://www.vanityfair.com/images/politics/2008/03/posl08_obama0803.jpg

http://www.newsweek.com/media/62/new-yorker-cover-obama-michelle-joke-vl.jpg

http://en.wikipedia.org/wiki/File:Lyndon_Johnson_signing_Civil_Rights_Act,_2_
July,_1964.jpg

HILLARY CLINTON

SOURCES:

http://www.biobble.com/fr/2006-563/Hillary_Clinton_biographie.html

http://www.nytimes.com/2007/09/05/us/politics/05clinton.html?_r=1&oref=slogin

http://www.youtube.com/watch?v=82qCwLX9piE

http://en.wikipedia.org/wiki/Hillary_Rodham_Clinton

http://en.wikipedia.org/wiki/List_of_U.S._states_by_population

http://en.wikipedia.org/wiki/List_of_female_United_States_presidential_and_vice-
presidential_candidates

http://en.wikipedia.org/wiki/Whitewater_controversy

http://www2.scholastic.com/browse/article.jsp?id=4647

http://en.wikipedia.org/wiki/Senate_career_of_Hillary_Rodham_Clinton

http://en.wikipedia.org/wiki/Rose_Law_Firm

http://en.wikipedia.org/wiki/Wellesley_College

http://en.wikipedia.org/wiki/Yale_Law_School

http://en.wikipedia.org/wiki/Chicago_metropolitan_area

http://en.wikipedia.org/wiki/Bill_Clinton

http://en.wikipedia.org/wiki/60_Minutes

http://transcripts.cnn.com/TRANSCRIPTS/0305/15/lkl.00.html

http://en.wikipedia.org/wiki/Clinton_health_care_plan

http://en.wikipedia.org/wiki/United_States_House_of_Representatives_elections,_1994

http://en.wikipedia.org/wiki/Barry_Goldwater

http://voices.washingtonpost.com/fact-checker/2007/12/hillary_and_martin_luther
king.html

http://en.wikipedia.org/wiki/Martin_Luther_King,_Jr.

http://en.wikipedia.org/wiki/Hillary_Rodham_cattle_futures_controversy

http://en.wikipedia.org/wiki/Arkansas_Advocates_for_Children_and_Families

IMAGES:

http://graphics8.nytimes.com/images/2007/09/05/us/05clinton.1-600.jpg

http://www.enquirer.com/editions/2000/05/04/ksu.jpg

http://brownsugarpages.files.wordpress.com/2008/04/mlk_jr_slaying.jpg

http://media.washingtonpost.com/wp-srv/photo/homepage/hp6-3-08uu.jpg

http://images.google.com/images?q=Clinton%20Inauguration&ie=UTF-8&oe=utf-
8&rls=org.mozilla:en-US:official&client=firefox-a&um=1&sa=N&tab=wi

http://clinton1.nara.gov/White_House/Family/images/raw/INAU26.GIF

http://cm1.theinsider.com/media/0/25/41/Monica_lewinsky.0.0.0x0.280x280.jpeg

http://www.chicagomag.com/images/2008/March%202008/politics_hillary.jpg

http://www.aliciapatterson.org/APF0804/Judis/Judis01.jpg

http://www.bbc.co.uk/radioassets/photos/2008/4/1/39373_2.jpg

http://farm1.static.flickr.com/25/40679205_d6805f1eeb.jpg

http://img129.imageshack.us/img129/3633/hillary1ic9.jpg

http://www.americanrhetoric.com/images/nixonresignation.JPG

http://media.ourstory.com/50/87/90/7a4bdd5ff51c1400f4d0b608b906cda41f35fcf7/6b
2af830a69c0ec2e0741af459522732277012b7.jpg

http://images.google.com/images?q=Arkansas&ie=UTF-8&oe=utf-8&rls=org.
mozilla:en-US:official&client=firefox-a&um=1&sa=N&tab=wi

http://www.historicaldocuments.com/JimmyCarter_BillClinton.jpg

SARAH PALIN

SOURCES:

http://news.sky.com/skynews/Home/World-News/Sarah-Palin-May-Have-Won-The-Debate-But-She-Isnt-Up-To-The-Job-Of-Vice-President/Article/200810115114465

http://en.wikipedia.org/wiki/Sarah_Palin

http://en.wikipedia.org/wiki/Political_positions_of_Sarah_Palin

http://en.wikipedia.org/wiki/Public_image_and_reception_of_Sarah_Palin

http://en.wikipedia.org/wiki/Wasilla,_Alaska

http://earthquakehelp.blogspot.com/2005/04/93-anchorage-alaska.html

http://pennsylvaniaforjohnmccain.blogspot.com/2008/03/sarah-palins-appeal-to-pennsylvanians.html

http://weeklystandard.com/content/public/articles/000/000/013/851orcjq.asp

http://www.hsmaps.com/dir/Alaska/WASILLA/WASILLA+HIGH+SCHOOL%5E%5E20 21%5E%5E

http://www.welcometoalaska.com/wasilla.htm

http://www.whs.matsuk12.us/

http://maps.google.com/maps?q=Wasilla+High+School&sll=61.5817,-149.466&s spn=1.279,4.01461&ie=UTF8&v=2.2&cv=4.3.7284.3916&hl=en&latlng=61588640,-149414427,108101733324901329160&ei=rK7_SJijCJ_KjAOk98CKDw&cd=1

http://hogwash.today.com/2008/08/30/sarah-palin-biography/

http://gov.state.ak.us/bio.html

http://www.youtube.com/watch?v=ddRoiVWfLyU

http://womensissues.about.com/od/genderwarriors/p/SarahPalin.htm

http://www.adn.com/sarah-palin/story/525556.html

http://www.cbsnews.com/blogs/2008/08/29/politics/horserace/entry4397867.shtml

http://tizona.wordpress.com/2008/02/26/mccains-perfect-choice-for-a-running-mate-governor-sarah-palin/

http://en.wikipedia.org/wiki/Mayoralty_of_Sarah_Palin

http://en.wikipedia.org/wiki/Governorship_of_Sarah_Palin#Public_Safety_Commissioner_dismissal

http://en.wikipedia.org/wiki/John_McCain_presidential_campaign,_2008

http://en.wikipedia.org/wiki/Alaska_Public_Safety_Commissioner_dismissal

http://en.wikipedia.org/wiki/Tesoro_Iron_Dog

http://en.wikipedia.org/wiki/Electoral_history_of_Barack_Obama

http://www.cnn.com/2008/POLITICS/09/11/palin.father/index.html

http://www.time.com/time/nation/article/0,8599,1849910,00.html

http://themoderatevoice.com/22747/quote-of-the-day-on-attempts-to-derail-palin-troopergate-investigation/

http://www.youtube.com/watch?v=wqBLUIJ-zYc&feature=related

http://www.cnn.com/2008/POLITICS/10/03/debate.poll/

http://elections.nytimes.com/2008/president/debates/transcripts/vice-presidential-debate.html

http://www.allvoices.com/contributed-news/1500949-palin-legs

http://blogs.wsj.com/washwire/2008/10/17/palin-touts-the-pro-america-areas-of-the-country/

http://www.cnn.com/2008/POLITICS/10/21/palin.sitroom/index.html

http://blog.mlive.com/mediumfidelity/2008/10/tina_fey_sarah_palin_redux_rea.html

http://www.clipsandcomment.com/2008/10/19/transcript-colin-powell-on-meet-the-press-endorses-barack-obama-october-19/

http://www.conservapedia.com/Sarah_Palin

http://www.foxnews.com/politics/elections/2008/09/02/obama-i-have-more-executive-experience-than-palin/

http://www.nydailynews.com/news/politics/republican_race/2008/09/01/2008-09-01_bristol_palins_pregnancy_was_an_open_sec.html

http://www.huffingtonpost.com/2008/11/05/sarah-palin-2012-sounds-s_n_141446.html

http://www.huffingtonpost.com/2008/10/21/rnc-has-spent-over-150000_n_136736.html

http://www.youtube.com/watch?v=z-kjM1asH-8

http://www.youtube.com/watch?v=t5sLz8ck_Pw

http://www.youtube.com/watch?v=E2d5JnTzoyQ

http://www.politico.com/news/stories/1008/14805.html

http://www.nydailynews.com/news/politics/republican_race/galleries/meet_vp_candidate_sarah_palin/meet_vp_candidate_sarah_palin.html

http://www.momlogic.com/2009/01/bristol_palin_teen_pregnancy_n.php

http://abcnews.go.com/TheLaw/MindMoodNews/story?id=6577965&page=1

PICTURES:

http://blog.changeandexperience.com/2008/09/sarah-palin-wikipedia.html

http://www.thehollywoodgossip.com/images/gallery/todd-palin.jpg

http://www.sarah-louise-palin.com/images/PalinFamily_2005sm.jpg

http://commons.wikimedia.org/wiki/File:Mountains_around_Wasilla_Alaska.jpg

http://cantwell.homestead.com/files/map_wasilla.jpg

http://www.firsttimealaska.com/admin/images/wasilla-where-the-iditarod-really-starts.jpg

http://images.google.com/imgres?imgurl=http://alaskarama.com/musc/front.jpg&imgrefurl=http://alaskarama.com/musc/&h=244&w=320&sz=16&hl=en&start=3&um=1&usg=__p1-LuNNbGT1mafj76TNwLhxlMaw=&tbnid=mEMRfpM49dju3M:&tbnh=90&tbnw=118&prev=/images%3Fq%3DWasilla%2BMulti-Use%2BSports%2BComplex%26um%3D1%26hl%3Den%26client%3Dfirefox-a%26rls%3Dorg.mozilla:en-US:official%26sa%3DN

http://opinionhead.com/wp-content/uploads/2008/06/oil-rig-alaska.jpg

http://ktuu.images.worldnow.com/images/8194634_BG3.jpg

http://hotlineblog.nationaljournal.com/Palin.bmp

http://www.wildlife.state.nh.us/Hunting/Moose_hunt/Moose_field_pics/Field_dressing.gif

http://en.wikipedia.org/wiki/File:Sarah_Palin_Kuwait_Crop2.jpg

http://images.huffingtonpost.com/gadgets/slideshows/611/slide_611_12581_large.jpg

CAROLINE KENNEDY

TEXTS:

"Sweet Caroline: Last Child of Camelot" (Christopher Andersen, Doubleday, 2003)

ARTICLES:

http://media.www.cm-life.com/media/storage/paper906/news/2003/11/21/Voices/Jfk-Assassinated-2491957.shtml

http://www.biography.com/articles/Caroline-Kennedy-204598

http://www.answers.com/topic/caroline-kennedy-schlossberg

http://womenshistory.about.com/od/writers20th/p/carolinekennedy.htm

http://www.foxnews.com/politics/2008/12/15/bio-caroline-kennedy/

http://www.infoplease.com/biography/var/carolinekennedyschlossberg.html

http://www.nytimes.com/2009/01/19/nyregion/19caroline.html?_r=2&fta=y&pagewanted=all

http://www.nytimes.com/1986/03/02/style/caroline-bouvier-kennedy-to-wed-edwin-schlossberg.html

http://gawker.com/5070555/new-rose-kennedy-schlossberg-photos-tell-shocking-tale-of-smoking-drinking-famous-college-student

http://www.arlingtoncemetery.net/jfk-112203.htm

http://www.nytimes.com/2008/01/27/opinion/27kennedy.html

MODIFIED VISUAL IMAGE REFERENCE SOURCES:

http://pro.corbis.com/images/WL002661.jpg?size=67&uid={F8187309-6DDE-4531-B976-0B932AA4A7F8}

http://farm3.static.flickr.com/2086/2131923107_59860cf110.jpg

http://www.theforbiddenknowledge.com/hardtruth/kennedy7.jpg

http://media.collegepublisher.com/media/paper906/stills/3fbd9114ebca4-13-1.gif

http://pro.corbis.com/images/U1379123B.jpg?size=67&uid={7d48c523-37b1-4f1b-b5f6-9a280287d50c}

http://theconcordlife.com/wp-content/uploads/2008/10/concord-academy3.JPG

http://storage.people.com/jpgs/19860317/19860317-750-0.jpg

http://photos.upi.com/topic/6b9159586055c0c4cdcd30d3e3f71684/Edwin_Schlossberg_1.jpg

http://upload.wikimedia.org/wikipedia/en/b/b1/Rose_kennedy.JPG

VIDEO:

http://www.youtube.com/watch?v=gOqkbHrD488

http://www.youtube.com/watch?v=RgEmll7qreo&

http://www.youtube.com/watch?v=LdMP_TKb0R8&

http://www.youtube.com/watch?v=ZQNTYc4Zsyl

WIKIPEDIA (cross referenced):

http://en.wikipedia.org/wiki/Caroline_Kennedy

http://en.wikipedia.org/wiki/State_funeral_of_John_F._Kennedy

http://en.wikipedia.org/wiki/John_F._Kennedy_assassination

http://en.wikipedia.org/wiki/Jacqueline_Kennedy_Onassis

http://en.wikipedia.org/wiki/Metropolitan_Museum_of_Art

http://en.wikipedia.org/wiki/Edwin_Schlossberg

http://en.wikipedia.org/wiki/Rose_Fitzgerald_Kennedy

http://en.wikipedia.org/wiki/John_F._Kennedy,_Jr.

http://en.wikipedia.org/wiki/Death_and_state_funeral_of_Gerald_Ford

http://en.wikipedia.org/wiki/Death_and_state_funeral_of_Ronald_Reagan